LAMBORGHINI

A SOURCE BOOK

EDITED AND ANNOTATED BY

Robert C. Ackerson

Motorbooks International
Publishers & Wholesalers Inc
Osceola, Wisconsin 54020, USA

Bookman Publishing/Baltimore, Maryland

Printed in the U.S.A.

ISBN 0-934780-37-4

First Edition
First Printing

Inquiries may be directed to:
Bookman Dan!, Inc.
P.O. Box 13492
Baltimore, Maryland 21203

Book trade distribution by:
Motorbooks International
P. O. Box 2
Osceola, Wisconsin 54020

Contents

The publishers would like to extend their special thanks to Z. Taylor Vinson, from whose private collection came most of the Lamborghini material reproduced in this book. Mr. Vinson has been of invaluable assistance in the research and preparation of other volumes in this series, as well, and his unfailing cooperation in the face deadline pressures and other various and sundry recurring horrors of the publishing trade has been much appreciated.

A PARITAL LISTING OF LAMBORGHINI
FACTORY-ISSUED SALES LITERATURE

1963 350 GTV folder (by Commercio-Bologna)
1964 350 GT sheet (by Commercio-Bologna)
1964 350 GT folder w/blue car (by Commercio-Bologna)
1965 350 GT folder w/silver car (by Commercio-Bologna)
1966 350 GT folder (A/1)
1966 400 GT 2+2 catalogue (B/1, by Commercio-Bologna)
1967 Miura P400 catalogue (M/1, w/o 40019 address on back)
1967 400 GT 2+2 catalogue (B/1, by Pettorali-Milano)
1968 Miura P400 catalogue (M/1, w/40019 address on back)
1968 Islero folder (by Commercio-Bologna)
1968 Espada folder (by Commercio-Bologna)
1968 Espada, Islero, Miura sheet
1969 Islero 400 GTS folder (by Commercio-Bologna)
1969 Miura S folder (M/1, by Commercio-Bologna)
1969 Espada, Islero S, Miura S folder (by Julia-Roma)
1970 Miura S folder (M/S, by Commercio-Bologna)
1970 Espada, Jarama, Miura S folder (by Renografica-Bologna)
1970 Espada catalogue (10-70, by Commercio-Bologna)
1971 Jarama catalogue (3-71, by Renografica-Bologna)
1971 Espada, Jarama, Miura SV folder
1972 Urraco P250 catalogue (by Renografica-Bologna)
1972-4 Espada, Jarama, Miura SV, Urraco P250, Jarama S, Countach small portfolio issued in various model combinations with blue, brown, green, gray, tan and yellow covers
1973 Espada catalogue (3-73, by Renografica-Bologna)
1973 Jarama S catalogue (by Commercio-Bologna)
1973 Urraco P250 catalogue (by Renografica-Bologna)
1974 Countach folder (by Renografica-Bologna)
1975 Urraco P300 catalogue (w/brown car, by Renografica-Bologna)
1976 Urraco P111 catalogue (by Renografica-Bologna)
1976 Countach catalogue (by ARBE-Modena)
1976 Espada catalogue (2-76, by Renografica-Bologna)
1976 Urraco P300 catalogue (w/yellow car, by Renografica-Bologna)
1977 Silhouette catalogue (by Stayer-Graph Granarolo)
1977 Urraco P300 catalogue (w/brown car, by Stayer-Graph Granarolo)
1977 Countach catalogue (by Stayer-Graph Granarolo)
1977 Espada catalogue (2-76, by Stayer-Graph Granarolo)
1981 Countach S portfolio
1981 Countach S folder
1982 Jalpa catalogue

Preface

Few automobile manufacturers have had as traumatic and sensational a history as has Lamborghini. Like Ferrari, its founder, Ferruccio Lamborghini was a man dedicated to excellence and precise manufacturing techniques who possessed an instinctive knowledge of what was or wasn't good design. But, unlike Enzo Ferrari, whose entire life was wrapped up in the construction, racing and development of automobiles, Lamborghini was an industrialist whose products, which included tractors, heating devices and air conditioners, were somewhat less spectacular. However, Lamborghini's efforts were immensely profitable and as a result he could afford to indulge himself with the purchase of exotic and expensive automobiles. As it has happened on more than one occasion, this passion could only be satisfied by the manufacture of an automobile bearing his name. Thus the first Lamborghini 350 GT came to production in 1964. But, the Lamborghini should never be thought of as if it were a mere counterpart to the Ferrari. Instead, from the very beginning it was a true alternative, possessing a personality unlike any other high-performance automobile. Moreover, Lamborghini soon became identified with advanced concepts that other manufacturers only dreamed about. Lamborghini, on the other hand, embraced them with open arms and to the admiration of any objective observer converted dreams and visions into production automobiles. Yet, at the same time, Lamborghini wasn't immune to the unforgiving forces of the real world of economics. Without the immense strength of Ferrari, Lamborghini, like Maserati and Aston Martin, fell upon hard times during the difficult years of the seventies. While the situation didn't reach the abysmal level of liquidation, it did see Lamborghini go from a position of considerable economic strength through a series of owners and receivership. Now, with a world-wide economic recovery and a stabilized fuel situation, it's more than likely that Lamborghini with its acclaimed reputation for innovation and glorious automobiles will return to financial health and success. It is in that perspective that this volume is presented, not as a requiem but as a prelude to even greater glories from Lamborghini.

A number of fine volumes on Lamborghini are currently available. Chris Harvey's "The Lamborghini From 350 GT to Jalpa," for example provides a concise overview of Lamborghini history. His effort plus contemporary road tests and articles from "Road & Track," "Car and Driver" and the British publications, "Autocar" and "Motor," were useful references. Other valuable information was drawn from material originally published by the Lamborghini factory.

The purpose of a Source Book is to tell the story of a car through use of the original manufacturer's literature, some of which, certainly in the case of Lamborghini, may be quite rare. A comprehensive listing of major items of Lamborghini sales literature is given at the end of each chapter. One or two of the most important items have, in each case, been selected for reproduction here and they are keyed in the text.

Schenevus, New York
April, 1984

Lamborghini

350 GT

It's been said that no matter how hard you pull on the neck of a duck, you won't end up with a swan. Be that as it may, more than one automobile has begun life as an ugly duckling only to end up as a very attractive motorcar. It's not inaccurate to consider the first Lamborghini 350 GTV in that context. When it was first displayed at the October 1963 Turin Show its Scaglione-designed body appeared as a hopeless mish-mash of dated styling cliches, more often than not in serious conflict with each other. None-the-less the 350 GTV possessed other impressive credentials strongly suggestive of an automobile with the potential to seriously challenge Ferrari's pre-eminent position among the world's exotic cars.

Its engine was an aluminum alloy (with cast iron liners), 60o V-12 fitted with four chain driven overhead cams, a 3.03 inch bore, 2.44 inch stroke and a displacement of 211 cubic inches or 3464 cc. A cast aluminum cylinder head (with hemispherical combustion chambers) was also fitted and the engine's 53.24 pound, 7 bearing crankshaft originated as a 204 pound billet.

All in all, this was an impressive beginning but by October 1964 when the London Automobile Show opened Lamborghini had determined the direction which he wanted his automotive venture to follow. The result was a vastly improved product. Touring, who in the interim has been given responsibility for the Lamborghini's appearance, removed its excessively fussy front and rear fender indentations, the non-harmonious side trim and the awkwardly formed rear lights and bumper. Also gone were the six exhaust pipes (replaced by four units) and the retractable headlights gave way to oval-shaped Cibie units that contributed much to the Lamborghini's very distinctive appearance. The least-pleasing aspect of this design remained its rear deck where the combination of undersized taillights, a very high rear window and an oversized indentation for the license plate gave the Lamborghini a tallish, narrow look. At the front there was just a hint of the Ferrari 275 GTB in the inward sweeping of the Lamborghini's fenders but beyond that probably coincidental similarity the two marques had little in common. The high-mounted, slightly inboard headlight pods trailed off into the hood, which without any scoops or vent had a very broad appearance. Early models by Touring had a simple mesh grille insert but later versions carried two chrome bars.

As expected, no major revisions were made in the V-12 Lamborghini engine. However, in the transformation from 350 GTV to 350 GT, the V-12's wet sump was replaced by a dry sump version and its six vertical twin-choke 361IDL Weber carburetors gave way to the same number of side draft, 40DCOE Webers. With twin electric fuel pumps (drawing fuel from two tanks with a total capacity of 21 gallons) and 9.5:1 compression ratio, the 350 GT engine was rated at 336 hp at 6500 rpm and 254 lb-ft of torque at 5700 rpm. A ZF, five-speed all-syncromesh transmission was fitted and a choice of 3.3, 3.5 and 3.8:1 rear axle ratios was offered.

The Touring body was constructed of aluminum and mounted upon a tubular, ladder type frame. As it had done for many years the Touring firm described this construction as "Superleggera." Beneath this skin was an up-to-date, all-independent suspension with upper and lower wishbones, anti-roll bars and coil springs with concentric shock absorbers at all four wheels. Up front, 11.5 inch disc brakes were used with 10.8 inch units at the rear. Front and rear tread was 54.5 inches and the 350 GT rode on 205x15 Pirelli Cinturato H. S. tires mounted on 6.5 inch Borrani wire wheels. A limited-slip differential was standard. Wheelbase was 96.5 inches and overall length was a trim 177 inches. The Lamborghini's width and height were 68.1 and 48 inches respectively.

The 350 GT was not promoted as a 2+2 but the storage area behind the front seats could, if needed, be used to accommodate two small children. For whatever reason it was used, this space was easily reached through the Lamborghini's very wide door openings. The twin leather covered bucket seats with built-in headrests were fully adjustable and were separated by a wide console. All pedals were suspended and a wood-rimmed, 3-spoke steering wheel with a charging bull logo was installed. Instrumentation was more than complete, it was awesome. A tachometer redlined at 7000 rpm and a speedometer reading to 300 Km/hr were positioned directly behind the steering wheel. Between them was a smaller gauge for the oil pressure. Four similarly-sized gauges for water temperature, gas, ammeter and oil temperature were positioned directly above the center console. Mounted above these instruments were seven tell-tale lights for the same number of toggle switches found midway on the console. Two of these (one in each end) operated the fresh air vents, those remaining controlled the wipers, panel lights, the ignition and cigarette lighter. The horn and directional signal controls were placed on a stalk protruding from the steering column.

The Lamborghini's performance was, as expected, exceptional. Its handling exhibited no vices and a top speed approaching 155 mph combined with a zero to 60 mph time of under seven seconds placed the 350 GT well within the realm of Ferrari's Grand Touring models.

Output of the 350 GT which listed in the United States for $13,900, was limited to just 131 units from 1964 to the cessation of production in 1967. In addition, two 350 GTV Lamborghinis were also turned out.

There were five main pieces of sales literature on the 350 GT. There were folders in 1963, 1964, 1965 (see pages 8-10) and 1966 (see pages 11-14). There was also a single sheet issued in 1964.

ideata per il gentleman che de

sidera stabilità, ripresa fulminea, frenatura docile e sicura

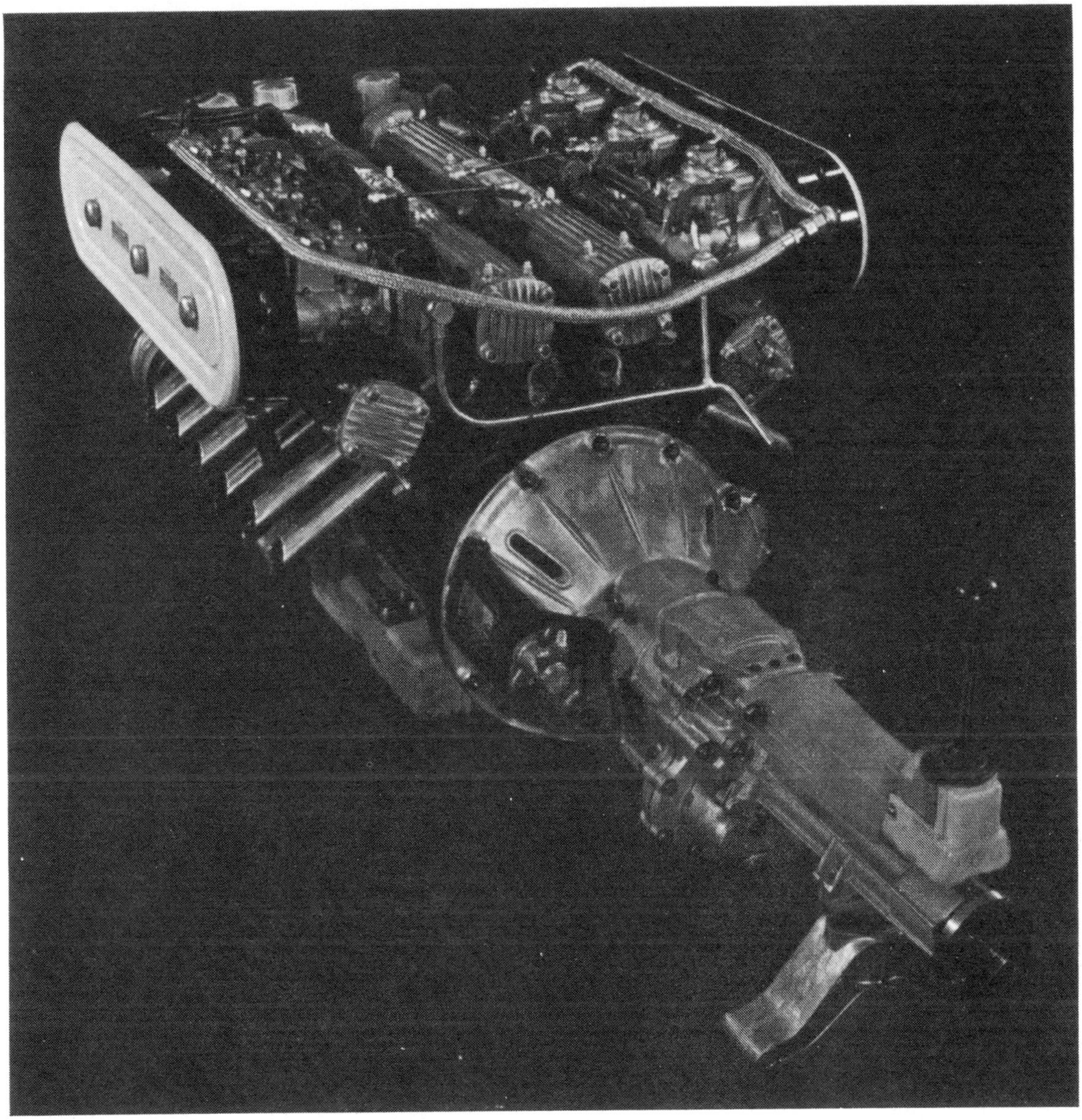

SPECIFICATIONS

Body 2 + 1 Seat Coupè
Overall Length 4,46 mt.
Overall Height 1,23 mt.
Overall Width 1,73 mt.
Engine 12 cylinders 60° V
Bore 77 mm - **Stroke** 62 mm
Displacement 3464 cc.
Compression Ratio 9 : 1
Max Power HP 280 DIN AT 6500 RPM
Block in aluminium alloy with shrunk in liners
Crankshaft Seven main bearings with 2 connecting rods per throw
Distribution 4 overhead camshafts Chain driven by 2 silent chains
Lubrification Gear type pump with full flow radiator and filter
Ignition 12 V. Battery coil with twin distributors
Cooling Centrifugal pump with 3 way flow radiator, 2 electric fans thermostaticaly controlled
Electrical System 12 V with 400 Watt alternator
Fuel system 6 twin choke weber carbs supplied by 2 electric fuel pumps
Clutch single dry plate hydraulic engagement
Gearbox ZF 5 speed + reverse fully synchronised
Differential Salisbury self locking
Chassis tubular construction with indipendent type front and rear suspensions equipped with coil springs telescopic shock absorbers and antiroll bars
Wheelbase 2,55 mt.
Track front 1,38 mt.
Track rear 1,38 mt.
Brakes double circuit discs on all 4 wheels with 2 vacumn servo units
Steering ZF worm-screw
Tyres 205 x 15 on Borrani spoked wheels
Fuel tank capacity 80 lt.
Fuel consumption lt. 16÷18 per 100 kms.
Max speed
with ratio 13/49 260 Km/h
with ratio 11/45 240 Km/h
with ratio 11/47 230 Km/h
Weight: Kg. 1200

TECNISCHE ANGABEN

Karosserie: 2 + 1 notsitz Kupee
Länge: 4,46 m.
Höhe: 1,23 m.
Breite: 1,73 m.
Motor: 12 Zylinder in 60° Winkelstellung
Bohrung 77 mm - Hub 62 mm
Zylinder-Inhalt: 3464 ccm.
Halbkugel-Verbrennungsraum.
Verdichtungsverh: 9 : 1
Höchstleistung bei 6500 Umdr/Min. 280 PS (DIN-Norm).
Motorblock: Leichtmetall mit aufliegenden Röhren
Antriebswelle: 7-fach gelagert, mit nebeneinanderliegenden Pleueln.
Kopfsteuerung: 4 durch geräuschlose Ketten mit Spanner betätigte Nocken-Wellen
Druckschmierung mit kompleter Filtrierung
Zündung: 12 V. Batterie u. 2 Verteiler
Kraftstoffzufuhr: 6 Weber-Doppelvergaser von 2 elektr. Pumpen gespeist
Wasserkühlung mit 2 elektrischen thermostatisch-gesteuerten Ventilatoren
Lichtanlage: Dynamo 12 V., 400 W.
Kupplung: einscheibentrockenkupplung hydraulisch betätigt.
Schaltgetriebe: 5 Vorwärtsgänge ZF m. Rückwärtsgang, vollsynchr.
Differential: Salisbury mit Selbstsperrung
Fahrgestell: Stahlrohrrahmen.
Radstand: 2,55 m.
Spurweite 1,38 m. vorn u. hinten.
Federung: Unabhängige Aufhängung der Vorder- und Hinterräder m. Spiralfedern
Teleskop-Stossdämpfern und Stabilisatorstangen
Scheibebremse mit Doppelkreis u. 2 Servobremsen
Lenkung: ZF
Räder: Gummibereifte Speichenräder 205 x 15
Benzintank: Inhalt 80 l.
Leistung:
Verbrauch (CUNA) 16÷18 l./100 Km.
Höchstgeschwindigkeit:
mit übersetzung 13/49 = 260 Km/h
mit übersetzung 11/45 = 240 Km/h
mit übersetzung 11/47 = 230 Km/h
Gewicht: 1200 Kg.

Tip. del Commercio - Bologna

400 GT 2+2

The rapid pace of evolution at Lamborghini was typified by the arrival of the 400 GT 2+2 in early March 1966. This model was easily set apart from the 350 GT by its dual headlight system and considerably smaller rear window. But, Lamborghini watchers could also detect its higher, by two inches, roofline and the altered rake of the windshield and backlight. Not as apparent were the all-new exterior body panels of the 400 GT 2+2. Also not easily noticed was the longer wheelbase of this new 2+2, which was 100.3 inches. Overall length now measured 184.5 inches. Since production of the new Lamborghini was expected to substantially exceed that of the 350 GT, a switch from aluminum to steel for body construction was made. This resulted in a slight increase in curb weight, now 2,734 pounds. With the exception of a larger trunk capacity, due to the adoption of a single 20 gallon fuel tank, and the addition of the small rear 2+2 seats, the new Lamborghini's creature comforts were essentially the same as before.

A larger 3.23 inch bore increased the V-12's displacement to 239.7 cubic inches (3929 cc). This added volume raised horsepower to 320 (DIN) at 6500 rpm. Maximum torque was now 276 ft-lb at 4500 rpm. No major changes were made in the Lamborghini's suspension but its status as a 2+2 necessitated stiffer springs and shocks plus altered wishbones at the rear.

Carried over from the 350 GT was the worm and cam steering with four turns, lock-to-lock. A point of justifiable pride for Ferruccio Lamborghini was the 400's new five-speed, all-synchromesh (including reverse) transmission and differential which replaced respective units purchased from ZF and Salisbury. Designed and built by Lamborghini, these new components joined the V-12 engine as prime examples of the 400 GT 2+2's thoroughbred character.

During its production run from 1966 to 1968, a total of 224 examples of the 400 GT 2+2 were produced. In the United States its price (in 1968) of $14,750 was more than competitive with corresponding models from Aston Martin, Ferrari and Maserati.

In addition to the 2+2 model, the four liter engine was also available in the two-seater body as the 400 GT. Twenty-three of these coupes were constructed, three with aluminum bodies, the remainder with steel bodywork.

There was very little literature issued on the 400 GT 2+2, basically two editions of a catalogue printed in 1966 and 1967, respectively. The later edition is reproduced here (see pages 16-22).

400 GT 2+2

frontale

Studiata nella parte anteriore per ottenere un'alta penetrazione all'aria per l'elevata velocità che può raggiungere, presenta una nuova sistemazione dei fari, ora doppi e affiancati con gli abbaglianti all'interno e gli anabbaglianti all'esterno, e con i fanalini di posizione collocati sui baffi dei paraurti realizzati in acciaio inossidabile.

Nella parte anteriore della carrozzeria, al limite della fiancata e appena sotto il parabrezza sono collocate due prese di aria protette da una grigliatura, che immettono direttamente un flusso d'aria nell'abitacolo, assicurando un facile e rapido ricambio ed una perfetta ventilazione.

interno

L'interno presenta una estrema confortevolezza e l'innovazione maggiore è data dalla capienza di quattro posti, molto comodi, che sono stati ottenuti abbassando leggermente il corpo telaio della vettura e alzando di 50 millimetri la curvatura del padiglione di carrozzeria.
I sedili anteriori, in pelle, sono due, anatomici e avvolgenti divisi fra loro dal pannello dei comandi e sono del tutto reclinabili.
I sedili posteriori, sempre in pelle, sono a divanetto.
I due cristalli laterali sono azionati elettricamente, mentre per i viaggiatori posteriori vi sono due deflettori dalla apertura a compasso. Le finizioni dell'arredamento interno sono di lusso.

plancia

La carenatura della plancia portastrumenti è stata realizzata all'insegna della sicurezza evitando ogni spigolatura e rivestendo il tutto di materiale imbottito. La plancia è sormontata da un'unghia in cuoio per annullare il riverbero degli strumenti sul parabrezza. Sulla plancia, da sinistra a destra il guidatore può trovare il contagiri, l'indicatore pressione olio, il contachilometro, l'indicatore temperatura olio, l'indicatore temperatura acqua, l'indicatore del livello benzina e l'amperometro. In un riquadro centralizzato, sopra la leva del cambio a cloche, sono sistemati tutti gli altri comandi. Due i vani portaoggetti: uno chiuso a cassetto sull'estrema destra della plancia, ed uno aperto sul tunnel fra i due sedili anteriori.

motore

La Lamborghini 400 GT 2+2 è azionata da un potente motore a quattro litri che rappresenta una chiara evoluzione rispetto al motore da tre litri e mezzo da cui deriva. Tutte le parti meccaniche della vettura sono state realizzate negli stabilimenti di Sant'Agata Bolognese. Per la prima volta, infatti, su questa macchina è montato un gruppo del cambio e un gruppo differenziale interamente progettati e realizzati dalla Lamborghini. La 400 GT 2+2 è una vettura che unisce ad una maggior velocità, potendo superare i duecentosettanta chilometri orari, anche una maggior sicurezza, avendo in sé una più elevata riserva di potenza.
L'efficienza delle parti meccaniche della vettura sono messe in risalto anche dalla concezione sportiva con cui è stato realizzato il motore che ha quattro alberi a cammes in testa, con camere di scoppio emisferiche, elevato rapporto di compressione (10,2/1); basso rapporto corsa/alesaggio 0,756; struttura interamente in alluminio; 7 supporti di banco.

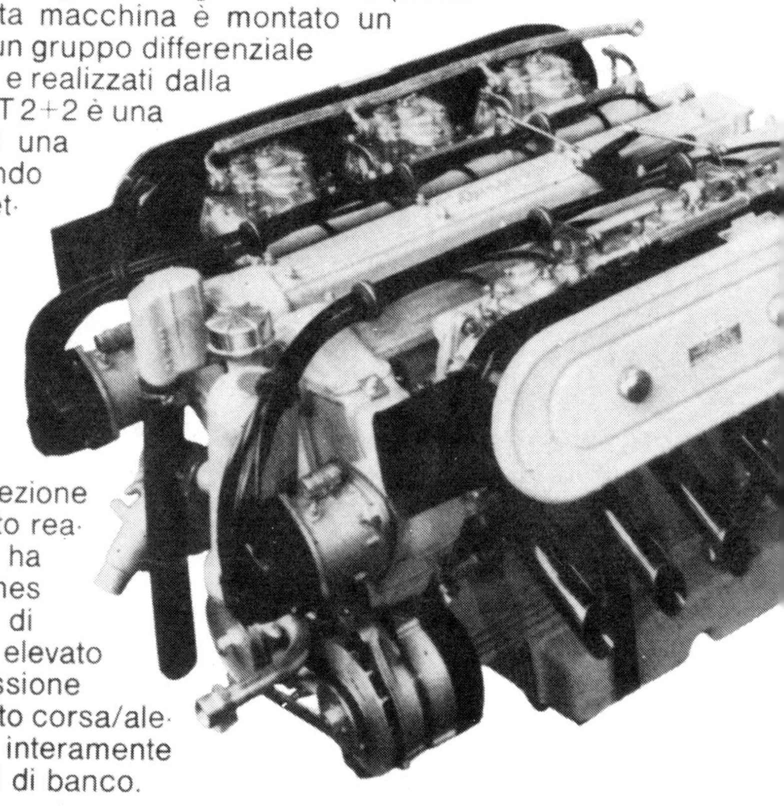

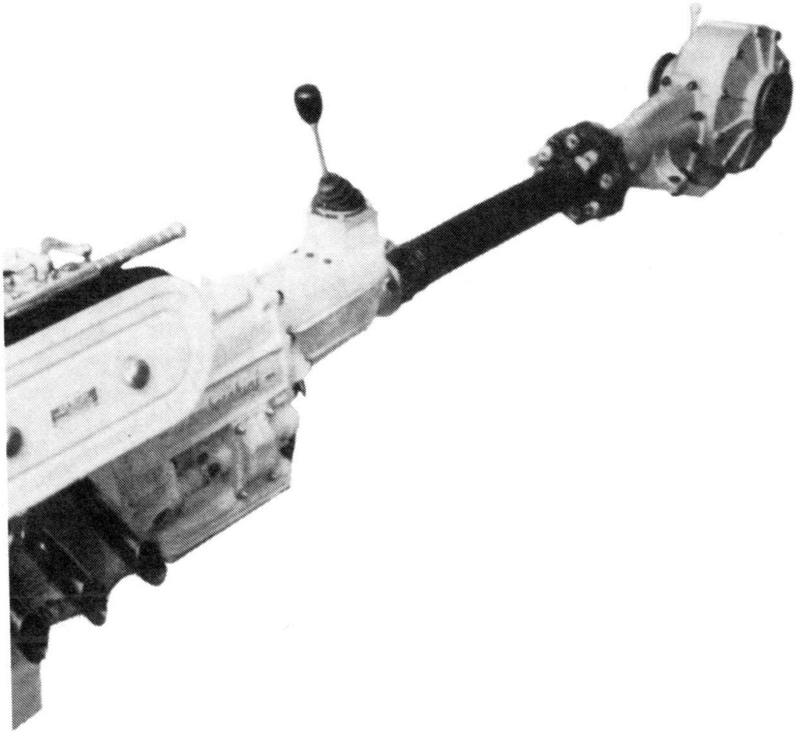

Specifications

Body: 2 + 2 Coupé
Overall Length 4,46 mt.
Overall Height 1.285 mt.
Overall Width 1,73 mt.
Engine: 12 cylinders 60° V
Bore 82 mm - Stroke 62 mm
Displacement 3929 cc.
Compression Ratio 10,2 : 1
Max Power HP 320 DIN AT 6500 RPM
Block in aluminium alloy with shrunk in liners
Crankshaft Seven main bearings with 2 connecting rods per throw
Distribution 4 overhead camshafts - Chain driven by 2 silent chains
Lubrification Gear type pump with full flow radiator and filter
Ignition 12 V. Battery coil with twin distributors
Cooling Centrifugal pump with 3 way flow radiator, 2 electric fans thermostatically controlled
Electrical System 12 V with 420 Watt alternator
Fuel system 6 twin choke Weber carbs supplied by electric fuel pump
Clutch single dry plate hydraulic engagement
Gearbox: Lamborghini 5 speed + reverse fully synchronised
Differential Lamborghini, 11/45
Chassis tubular cinstruction with indipendent type front and rear suspensions equipped with coil springs telescopic shock absorbers and antiroll bars
Wheelbase 2,55 mt.
Track front 1,38 mt.
Track rear 1,38 mt.
Brakes double circuit discs on all 4 wheels with 2 vacumn servo units
Steering ZF worm-screw
Tyres 205 x 15 on Borrani spoked wheels
Fuel tank capacity 87 lt.
Fuel consumption lt. 16 ÷ 18 per 100 Kms.
Max speed 270 Km/h
Weight: Kg. 1300

Miura

Just three years after its creation, Automobili Ferruccio Lamborghini SpA stunned the automotive world with the Lamborghini Miura. This automobile was, from virtually every point of analysis, a tour de force. Unlike the Ferrari 275LM, this was a true road sports car, not a relatively crude derivative of a pure racer. This didn't diminish the Ferrari's appeal, but it was a big plus for the Lamborghini.

Development of the Miura began in late 1964 and approximately one year later, in November 1965, a base chassis was displayed at the Turin Salon. The motoring world had its first look at the Miura's sensational styling at the March 1966 Geneva show. In effect, the final stages of the Miura's development were taking place while these displays intended to pique the potential customer's interest were taking place. Thus, by the October 1966 Paris Salon the Miura had changed substantially from its initial form. The original 96.9 inch wheelbase was stretched to 98.5 inches and the battery had been moved from the central frame tunnel to the front compartment. The placing of a V-12 engine transversely behind the driver and passenger posed major noise and heat problems for the Miura's designers, who soon abandoned the sloping rear window of the prototype for a series of slats through which engine heat and noise exited. To adequately insulate the Miura's occupants from uncomfortable sound and heat levels (but by nomeans to the deprivation of the enthusiast who thrived on the sound of a thoroughbred engine) a double-thickness "Visarm" plexiglass vertically positioned window was positioned directly in front of the engine. Also installed on an aluminum bulkhead between the engine and interior was a four inch layer of polystyrene.

These refinements were essential to the Miura's commercial success but the first ingredient in its recipe for modern classic status was its styling. With a 41.5 inch height and 171.5 inch overall length, the Miura's steel body flowed from front to rear in a series of voluptuous curves accentuated by several well-integrated grilles and vents. The talent behind this creation was Marcello Gandini, then in the employ of Nuccio Bertone. At the front a very wide and low grilled opening carried the directionals plus twin driving lights that could be flashed by the driver when desired. In place of the almost-expected concealed headlight system, the Miura was fitted with exposed Carello headlamps that blended into the front fender line when not in use. When needed they were moved, via electric motors, into the proper position. Surrounding the lights was a gridwork that directed air to the front brakes. Placed across the hood close to its leading edge were twin grilles that released hot air from the radiator. The right side unit also opened to provide access to the gas filler cap for the 25 gallon fuel tank. The Miura's windshield was sharply sloped and its thin side pillars were placed well back away from the driver's field of vision. Incorporated into the door's upper rear portion were vents that funneled air into the engine compartment, thus helping to force engine heat and exhaust out through the slats. The silver rocker panel ended in a smoothly sculptured scoop which directed air to the rear brakes. The rear view of the Miura was dominated by the back window venetian blinds. Just the slightest hint of a spoiler was found on the upper end of the tail section which surrounded the taillights, licence plate indent and black finished rear bumpers. External identification was limited to Miura script on the rear deck, a Lamborghini emblem on the front hood and a Bertone logo positioned just behind the doors. Campagnolo 15x7 magnesium alloy knock-off wheels with five large cooling scoops were fitted with GR70VR-15 Pirelli Cinturato HS tires rated for continuous operation at 165 mph.

Beneath this elegant form was a platform frame with deep sills and a center tunnel. Front and rear extensions served as supports for the suspension and engine components. The weight of the Miura frame was only 155 pounds. The suspension system of steel pressing wishbones and coil springs with concentric Armstrong shock absorbers was adapted from the early front-engined Lamborghini 350 GT, 400 GT and 400 GT 2+2 models. At the front a 0.75 inch anti-roll bar was fitted, with a 0.575 version found at the rear. Rack and pinion steering was used which provided 3.25 turns lock-to-lock.

The heart and soul of the Miura was, of course, its magnificent V-12 engine mounted transversely behind the cockpit. In most details it was similar to the 600 V-12 installed in earlier models. An aluminum block was used with wet cylinder liners and four chain-driven overhead cams. Total displacement was 3929 cc. But even seasoned Lamborghini enthusiasts were taken aback by the single aluminum casting for the Miura's engine block, crankcase, transmission and differential! A single plate Borg & Beck clutch transferred power through the Lamborghini-built, five-speed all-synchromesh gearbox to a ZF limited slip differential. The standard rear axle ratio was 4.65:1, other ratios available were 4.33 and 4.05:1.

The Miura engine was rated at 350 hp with a 9.5:1 compression ratio. Readily available was a "Sprint" version with a gross horsepower rating of 430 at 8000 rpm. This claimed output was always suspect but there's little doubt that with a 10.2:1 compression ratio and cams with 900 of overlap it was certainly capable of an output approaching 400 net horsepower. Both versions were equipped with six vertically mounted Weber 461DA3C, three barrel carburetors. Each engine was test-run for a 20 to 24 hour time span. The transmission evaluation lasted 12 hours.

Directly behind the wood-rimmed steering wheel was a Jaeger speedometer with a maximum 200 mph shown and an equal-sized, zero-to-10,000 rpm tachometer. The center panel was occupied by six smaller dials for water and oil temperature, oil pressure, fuel level and ammeter. Positioned below these instruments were nine lights serving as either warning or operating signals for such items as headlights, high beams, alternator, auxiliary cooling fan, etc. Located above the rear-view mirror were six switches controlling the single speed heater, ventilator fan, radiator fan (one unit operated automatically via a thermostat, the second was driver controlled) and for the head, fog, dash and panel lights. Located between the twin leather seats were ventilation ports that adjusted for both volume and direction. These also supplied heat if a water tap located under the dash was operated. Interior air vented through exits mounted across the back of the roof.

Although no independent Miura road test ever reached the 198 mph maximum claimed by the factory for the Sprint-engined Miura, there is ample evidence that it was one of the fastest road cars available. The "Motor" (August 1970) recorded a 171 mph top speed with a 350 hp Miura, which obviously needs no apologies. When production ceased in 1975 a total of 900 Miuras had been completed, no mean achievement for a car that in 1967 retailed for $19,250.

There was basically only one Miura P400 catalogue, in two slightly different editions (see pages 24-30).

Quadro portastrumenti

La guida sportiva richiede e impone una strumentazione completa e di agevole lettura: il cruscotto del Miura permette al pilota di avere costantemente sotto controllo la vettura, con strumenti e comandi disposti in modo razionale.

Perfetta linea sportiva

Aerodinamica, estremamente bassa (1055 millimetri) compatta e diffusamente studiata alla galleria a vento, la carrozzeria del MIURA P400 è la più moderna e razionale. Non meno affascinante di una macchina da corsa, la nuova vettura assicura una eccezionale penetrazione dell'aria.

Chassis

E' costruito in sottile lamiera di acciaio e disegnato in modo da formare una struttura particolarmente rigida e robusta; il motore è posto davanti all'asse posteriore, secondo i dettami dell'esperienza agonistica; le sospensioni sono indipendenti sulle 4 ruote, lo sterzo è a cremagliera.

Specifications

Coachbody

2 seater club coupé
Sheet steel and light alloy construction
Front and rear dumper hoods
Spare wheel, battery and tool kit in the front van
Headlights partly retractable
Dynamical air intakes drawn from the main section of the car

Chassis

In boxed and light weight sheet
Overall length mm. 4360
Overall width mm. 1760
Overall height mm. 1055
Wheelbase mm. 2500
Track (front and rear) mm. 1412

Mechanics

12 cylinders 60° V engine with gearbox and differential built into the same block
Block in aluminium alloy
Power 350 CV DIN at 7000 RPM
Compression ratio: 9,8 : 1
Crankshaft seven main bearings with connecting rods per throw.
Distribution 4 overhead camshafts
Fuel system with 4 triple body Weber carburettors
Two coil ignition system
Forward mounted water radiator with two thermosstatically controlled fan
Lamborghini gearbox with 5 speeds plus reverse, all synchronized
Differential self locking
Brakes: twin circuit Girling discs on the 4 wheels
Rack steering.
Suspension indepedent on the 4 wheels with telescopic Shock-absorbers
Wheels 7.00x15 Atesia alloy
Tyres: Pirelli HS Cinturato 210 x 15

Performances

Maximum speed:
300 Km/h road version
Fuel consumption CUNA 17-19 lt. per 100/Km.
Weight 980 Kg.

Miura S

In both 1969 and 1971 Lamborghini unveiled more powerful and refined versions of the Miura. The first of these, the Miura S, carried "Miura S" identification script on the right side of its rear deck. Justifying this new designation were several major engine and interior appointment changes. With reshaped combustion chambers, four Weber 40IDL-3L carburetors, higher lift cams and improved breathing, the Lamborghini V-12 developed 370 (net) hp at 7700 rpm. Maximum torque was 286 lb-ft at 5000 rpm. These changes enabled the Miura S to reach a maximum speed between 168 and 170 mph in contemporary road tests.

A new re-routed exhaust system allowed for a modest increase in luggage space and higher quality materials were used for the Miura's vinyl seats and carpeting. Included in the $19,250 price of the Miura S were electric window lifts. Air conditioning was available as an $800 option. Replacing the overhead toggle switches were rocker versions and the speedometer fitted to the Miura S had a maximum 190 mph reading. Indicative of the Miura's status as one of the most versatile of exotic cars was the 0.85G lateral acceleration figure recorded by "Road & Track" with a Miura S. This was unequalled by any car tested by "Road & Track" up to that time (April 1970).

Miura S folders were issued in 1969 and 1970. The later item is reproduced here (see pages 32-38).

MIURA S

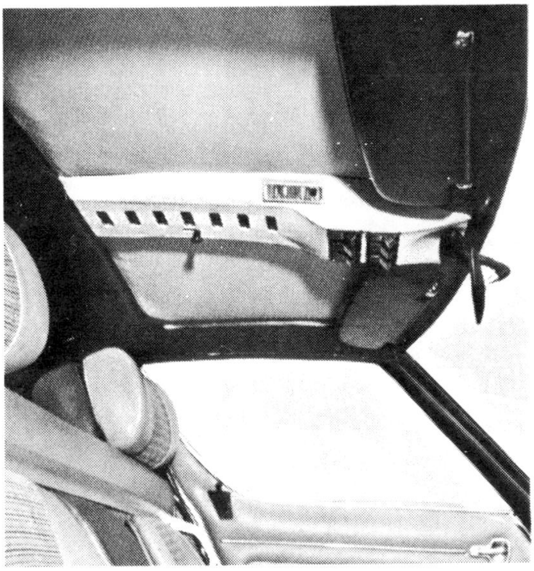

MIURA S

Specifications

Bodywork: 2 seater Berlinetta (Bertone)
Articulated front and rear shape
Spare wheel and batterie housed in the front van
Retractable halogen headlights
Electrically operated windows
Tinted glasses
Engine, transmission: V 12 (60°) inboard transverse rear engine in unit with differential and gearbox
Capacity 3929 cm^3 (82 x 62 mm)
Compression ratio 10,5 : 1
Maximum power: 370 bhp at 7700 rpm
Max. torque: 39,5 mkg (289 f.lbs.) at 5500 rpm
Light alloy cylinderblock and heads
7 crankshaft bearings
2 x 2 overhead camshafts
Single ignition system operated by 2 x 1 distributors
Cooling system: transverse flow radiator and twin electrical fans
Lamborghini 5 speed + reverse all syncromesh gearbox
Constant velocity half shafts
Electrical equipement: 12 V - batterie 72 Ah - alternator 450 W
Chassis: Monocoque steel bodywork
Front and rear indipendent suspension by double transverse wishbones: coil springs and telescopic shock absorbers
Girling twin braking system with ventilated discs on 4 wheels and rear pressure rise valve
Magnesium 7" x 15" rims
Tires: Pirelli Cinturato HS GR/70-VR 15
Dimensions: weight:
Wheelbase: 2504 mm (98.5")
Track front and rear: 1412 mm (55.6")
Lenght: 4390 mm (172.8")
Width: 1780 mm (70")
Height: 1100 mm (43")
Unladen weight (with oil and coolant): 1125 kg (2480 lbs.)
Performances: Top speed; 300 km/h (186 mph.)
Acceleration on 1 standing km: 23,2 sec.

Miura SV

The Miura SV (Super Veloce) which was introduced at the 1971 Geneva Show was distinguished by its nine-inch wheels, Pirelli Cinturato, FR70VR-15 low-profile tires, larger rear wheel cut outs and chrome door handles. With a higher, 10.7:1 compression ratio, its maximum horsepower rating was boosted to 385 at 7850.

The only Miura SV literature was a plate in a small full-line portfolio issued in 1972. It is reproduced here (see page 40).

miura
SV

Motore: 12 V (60°)
Cilindrata totale: 3929 cm^3
Rapporto di compressione: 10,7 : 1
Potenza max: 40,7 Kgm (Din)
N° giri max: 7850 g./min.
Posizione motore: centrale trasversale
Cambio: a 5 marce+RM
Sospensioni: a quattro ruote indipendenti con bracci trasversali
N° posti: 2
Peso a secco: 1245 Kg.
Velocità max: 290 km/h
Accelerazione (1 km da fermo) 24"

Engine: V 12 (60°)
Capacity: 3929 cm^3
Compression ratio: 10,7 : 1
Maximum power: 385 bhp
Max. torque: 40,7 lmkg (289 f. lbs.)
Max. R.p.m.: 7850
Transverse rear engine
Gearbox: 5 speeds + reverse
Suspension: front and rear indipendent with double transverse wishbones
n. Seats: 2
Dry weight: 1245 Kg. (2840 lbs.)
Top speed: 290 km/h
Acceleration (1 standing km: 24")

Moteur: V 12 (60°)
Cylindrée 3929 cm^3
Rapport de compression: 10,7:1
Puissance maxi: 40,7 mkg (DIN)
Position moteur: centrale arrère transversale
N° vitesses: 5+MA
Suspensions: quatre roues indépendentes guidées par leviers transversaux superposés
N° places: 2
Poids à sec: 1245 Kg.
Vitesse maxi: 290 Km/h
Accélération sur 1 km. 24"

Motor: V 12 (60°) 3929 cm^3
Verdichtung: 10,7 : 1
Höchstleistung: 385 PS bei 7850 U/Min
Max. Drehmoment: 40,7 mkg (Din)
Querliegender Heckmotor
Getriebe: 5 + R
Vorn und hinten Einzelradaufhängung durch Trapezquerlenker geführt
2 - Sitziges Berlinetta
Trockengewicht 1245 kg,
Höchstgeschwindigkeit: 290 km/h
Beschleunigung (auf 1 Km mit stehendem Start 24")

lamborghini

Islero

Produced in far fewer numbers than the Espada, which was introduced almost concurrently, the Islero represented the final form of Lamborghini's original front-engined grand touring concept. Mechanically it was virtually identical to the 400 GT 2+2. However, larger front and rear anti-roll bars were fitted and the Islero's overall length was five inches shorter than that of the 400 GT. Providing the Islero with an important performance edge over the older model was its lighter—by approximately 240 pounds—weight. Road test results indicated its top speed was an outstanding 161 mph. A limited-slip differential was standard with 11.8 inch and 11.0 inch disc brakes at the front and rear wheels, respectively. Pirelli Cinturato G70VR15 tires were mounted on seven inch Campagnolo knock-off, alloy wheels.

The interior arrangement of the early Islero models placed most gauges in a readable, if somewhat haphazard, arrangement. Later versions were far neater with the large tachometer and speedometer, separated by an oil temperature gauge, placed directly before the driver. The remaining five gauges (fuel, ammeter, oil pressure, water temperature and clock) were lined up in the same dash cove. Superseding the Islero's original push-pull switches were safer, rocker-type versions. Also abandoned was the original three spoke, wood-rimmed steering wheel in favor of a simpler, two spoke model. The passenger's dash bar was no longer installed. An elegant center console with Lamboghini Islero identification was a key feature of the Islero's interior redesign.

The styling of the Islero represented a sharp departure from the 400 GT's highly original and controversial design. By contrast, the Islero was more conservatively styled by Marazzi, who had picked up 400 GT 2+2 production after the demise of Touring. Only a wide chrome rocker panel bar and the wrap-around edges of the Islero's high-mounted front and rear bumpers graced its profile. Retractable headlights, a simple, center-positioned hood-scoop and a straight forward grille-opening housing supplementary road lights gave the Islero a marked similarity to the contemporary Maserati. However, a very large rear window, an aggressive fender line and a distinctive rear end with rectangular taillights placed beneath the two-piece bumper gave the Islero an overall look unshared by its peers.

Production of the $20,000 Islero spanned the years from 1967 to 1970. A total of 225 were built including a number of Islero S versions with more powerful, 350 hp (instead of 320 hp) engines.

There were at least two Islero folders issued, one on the Islero and one on the Islero S. The earlier version is reproduced here (see pages 42-48).

ISLERO

Lamborghini

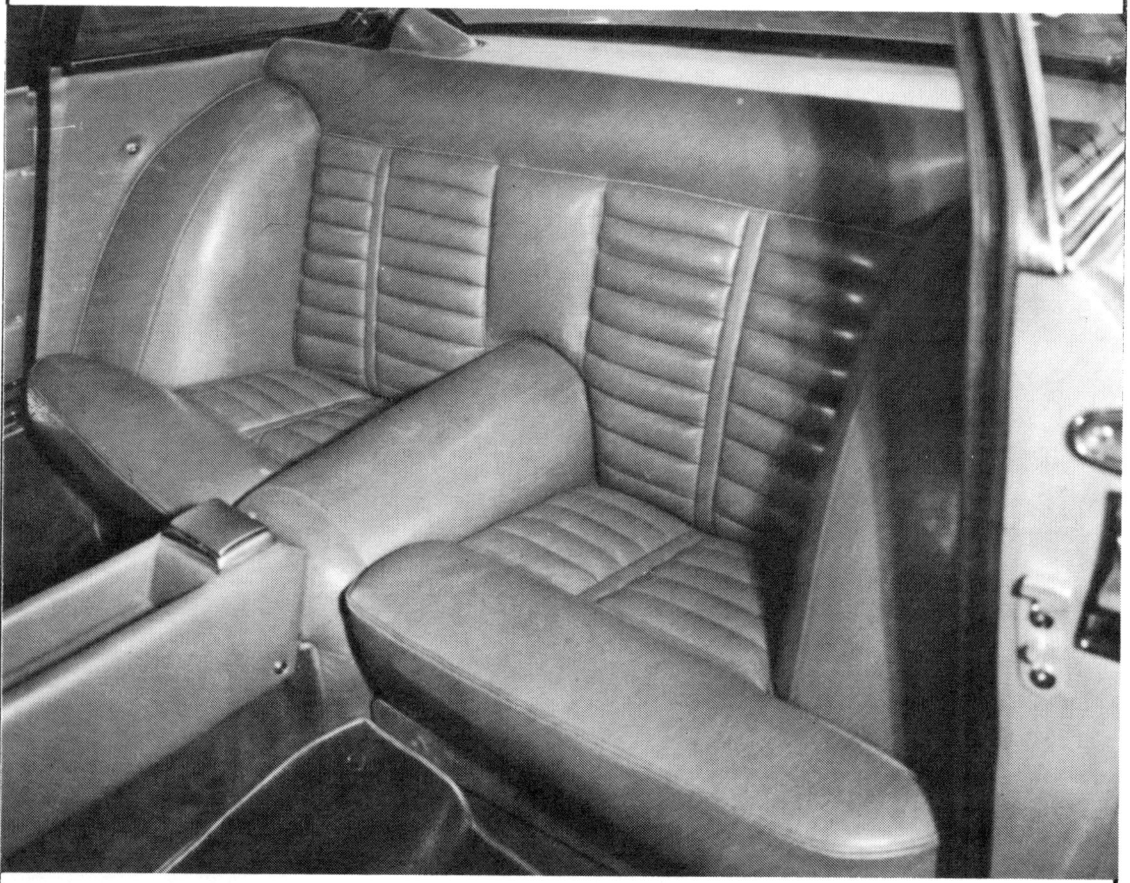

ISLERO
BP
è una Lamborghini!

potente veloce elegante

Specifications

Body: 2+2 Coupé
Overall length: 4.525 m. (178.1")
Overall height: 1.270 m. (50.0")
Overall width: 1.730 m. (68.1")
Engine: 60 V-12, dohc
Bore 82 mm - Stroke 62 mm
Displacement: 3929 cc
Compression ratio: 9.5:1
Bhp @ rpm: 320 DIN @ 6500
Block in aluminium alloy with shrunk in liners
Crankshaft: seven main bearings with two connecting rods per crank
Distribution: 4 overhead camshafts, chain driven by two silent chains
Carburetion: 6 Weber 40 DCOE 2V
Clutch: hydraulically operated single dry plate
Gearbox: Lamborghini 5 speed + reverse, synchromesh
Differential: Lamborghini 11:45
Frame: tubular
Independent front and rear suspension with coil springs, telescopic shock absorbers and anti-roll bars
Wheelbase: 2.55 m (100.3")
Track, front and rear: 1.38 m (54.3")
Brakes: discs on all four wheels, dual circuit, with two vacuum servo units
Steering: ZF worm and cam
Spoked or magnesium wheels with 205 x 15 tires
Fuel tank capacity: 85 l. (22.4 US. gal.)
Performances:
Fuel consumption: 16÷18 l per 100 km (CUNA)
Top speed: 265 km/h (165 mph)
Weight: 1220 kg (2795 lb)

Espada

When the forerunner of the Lamborghini Espada, the 2-liter Marzal first appeared at the 1967 Geneva Salon, both Lamborghini and Bertone insisted it was not a production prototype. The controversy surrounding this car's transparent, gullwing doors and unusual honeycombed rear window overshadowed the substantial advantage in the design of high-performance, luxury four-seater automobiles it represented. However, when the Espada entered into production in 1968 its importance as a 150 mph luxury four-seater was quickly comprehended. Unlike the Marzal, whose six-cylinder engine was mid-ship positioned, the front-engined Espada was powered by Lamborghini's 3929 cc V-12 rated at 320 DIN hp at 4500 rpm. Carburetion was by six 40DCOE, two-barrel Webers and a 9.5:1 compression ratio was claimed. In 1969, the introduction of the Series II Espada was highlighted by the use of the 350 hp Islero S engine as its standard power plant. Both engines as well as the Espada's five-speed transmission and the ZF limited-slip differential were virtual twins to those used in the Islero. Since the Espada was a luxury sports car, its all-independent suspension was fitted with softer springs and shock absorbers than the Islero. Smaller anti-roll bars were also installed. A wheelbase of 104.3 inches and an overall length of 185.8 inches made the Espada the longest Lamborghini yet constructed. Overall height was 46.4 inches and the Espada's width was 71.2 inches. Thus by way of comparison to the older 400 GT 2+2, the Espada was three inches wider and 4 inches lower. This provided for an interior fitted with four seats (those in the rear were identical to the front units except for the absence of adjustable back rests) and ample leg and luggage room.

The early production models were fitted with an interior dominated by an amazing array of geometric shapes, few of which were circular. The Series III Espada, introduced in 1973, had a revised dash panel which placed all instrumentation in a curved cove behind the steering wheel. The secondary switches were placed on the console. Most of the angles of the older version were removed from the Series III interior. Also offered, beginning in 1973, was Chrysler's three-speed Torqueflite automatic transmission.

Even after production of the Espada (which totalled nearly 900 cars) ceased in 1978, its styling was far from dated. Its low profile featured large side windows providing both excellent interior vision and a light, airy appearance. Small interior exhaust vents were installed on the rear quarter panel while unobtrusively narrow vents for engine heat were blended into the mid-body line crease. Twin NACA hood ducts served to direct air to the carburetors. Dual headlights were installed in the outer section of the grille opening which on the last models was covered by a black grille mesh.

The rear view of the Espada featured a unique, two-level window arrangement. A slatted, vertical window was installed directly beneath the nearly horizontal hatchback window.

At least ten items of sales literature were issued for the Espada making it the most "published" Lamborghini of all time. A comprehensive listing appears on page 4. Two brochures have been reproduced here, including a 1968 folder (see pages 50-56) and a 1973 catalogue (see pages 57-66).

ESPADA

ESPADA
BP
una creazione Lamborghini

la "4 posti" sportiva

Specifications

Body: coupé
Overal length: inches 185,0
Overall width: inches 71,6
Overall heigt: inches 46,8
Engine: 12 cylinders in « V » formation 60°
Bore: mm. 82
Stroke: mm. 62
Cubic capacity: cc. 3929
Hemispherical combustion chambers
Compression ratio: 9,5 : 1
Max Power: 325 HP DIN at 6,500 R.P.M.
Block in aluminium alloy with shrunk in liners
Crankshaft: Seven main bearings with 2 connecting rods per crank
Distribution: 4 overhead camshafts, driven by 2 silent chains
Forced lubrication - total draining
Ignition: by twin coils and distributor
Fuel system: 6 twin choke Weber carburettors fed by electric fuel pump
Water cooling system with centrifugal pump and two thermostatically controlled electric fans
Electrical system: 12 V with 600 Watt alternator
Clutch: single dry plate with hydraulic drive
Gearbox: Lamborghini 5 speed and reverse synchronized
Differential: Lamborghini 11/45
Chassis: tubular construction
Wheel base: inches 104,3
Ground front and rear level track: inches 58,6
Suspension: Front and rear: independent, coil spring, telescopic dampers and stabilizing bars
Brakes: discs on all 4 wheels in dual circuit with 2 vacuum servo units
Steering: ZF worm screw
Tyres: 205 x 15
Wheels: in magnesium alloy
Fuel tank capacity: Imp. galons 21
Normal consumption: 16÷18 lt. per 100 Kms.
Maximum speed: M.P.H. 152
Weight: 3262 lbs.
Conditioned air and heater fitted in the car

EE 0
2371

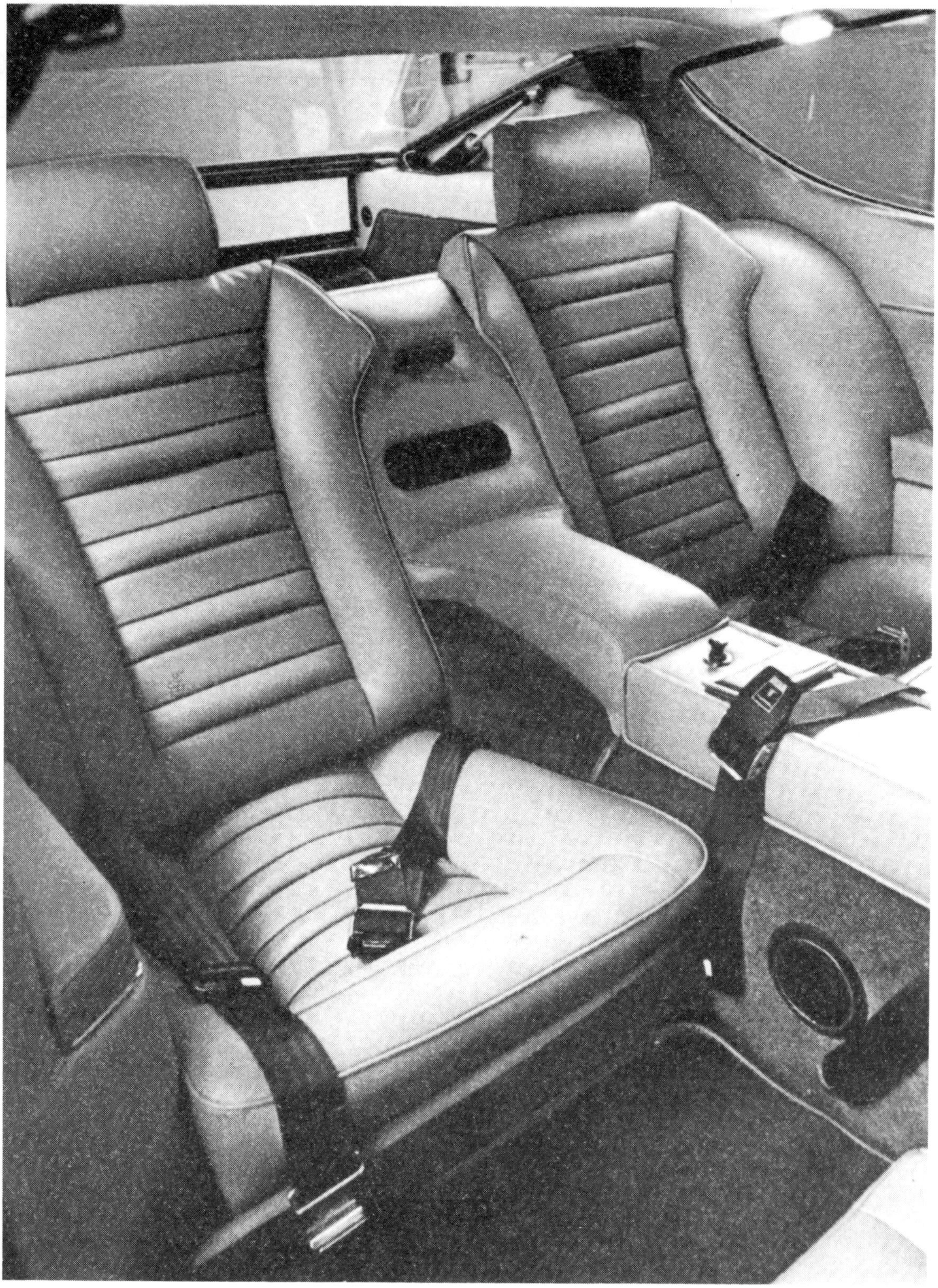

Al vertice
della perfezione meccanica:
12 cilindri a V,
4 assi a camme in testa,
6 carburatori
doppio corpo.

Uu sommet
da la perfection mécanique:
12 cylindres en V,
4 arbres à cames en tête,
6 carburateurs doubles.

Ins Heisse:
12 Zylinder in V-Bauart,
4 obenliegende Nockenwellen
6 Doppelvergaser.

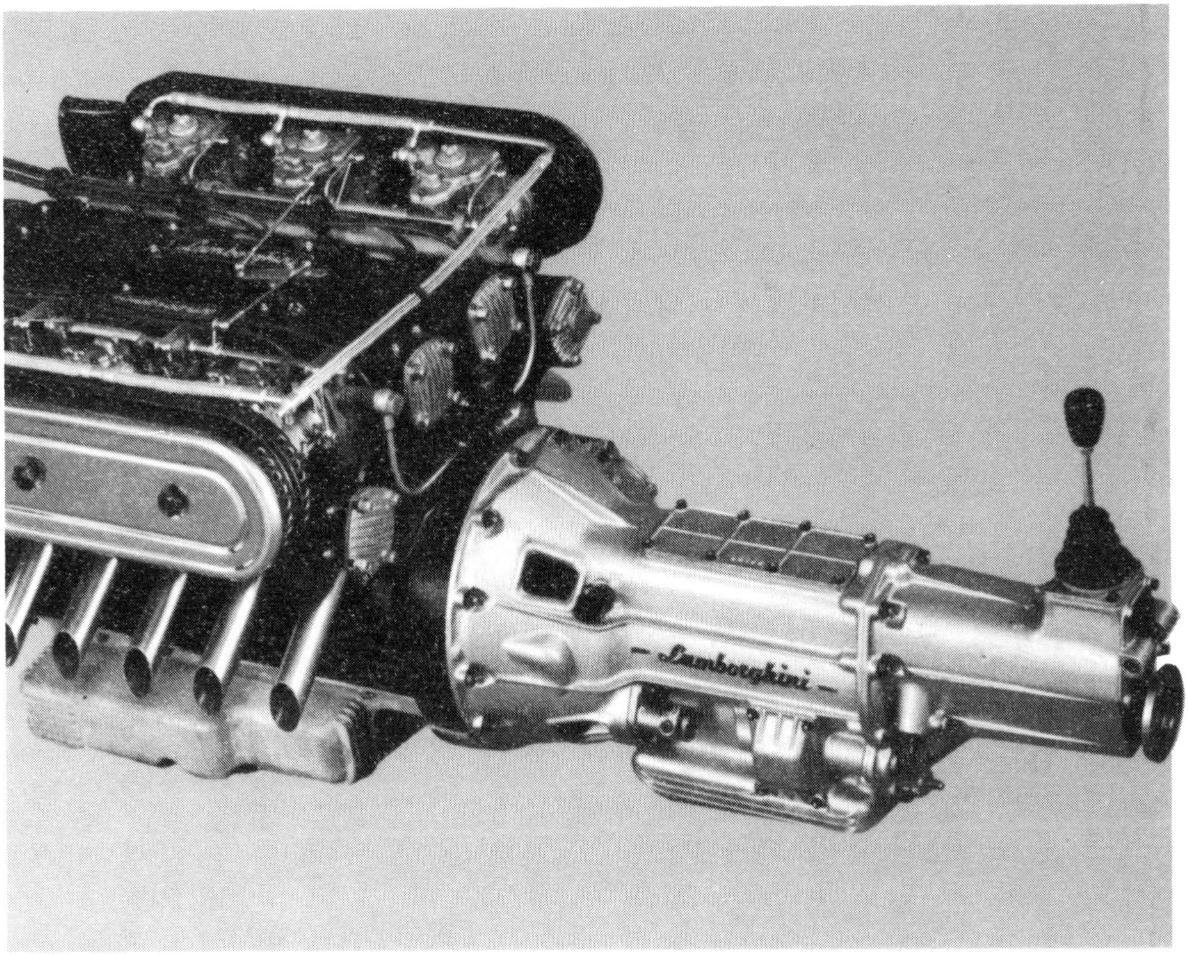

A top choice
in advanced engineering;
a big 240 cubic inch,
350 horsepower V-12 engine
with 4 overhead camshafts
and 6 twin carburetters.

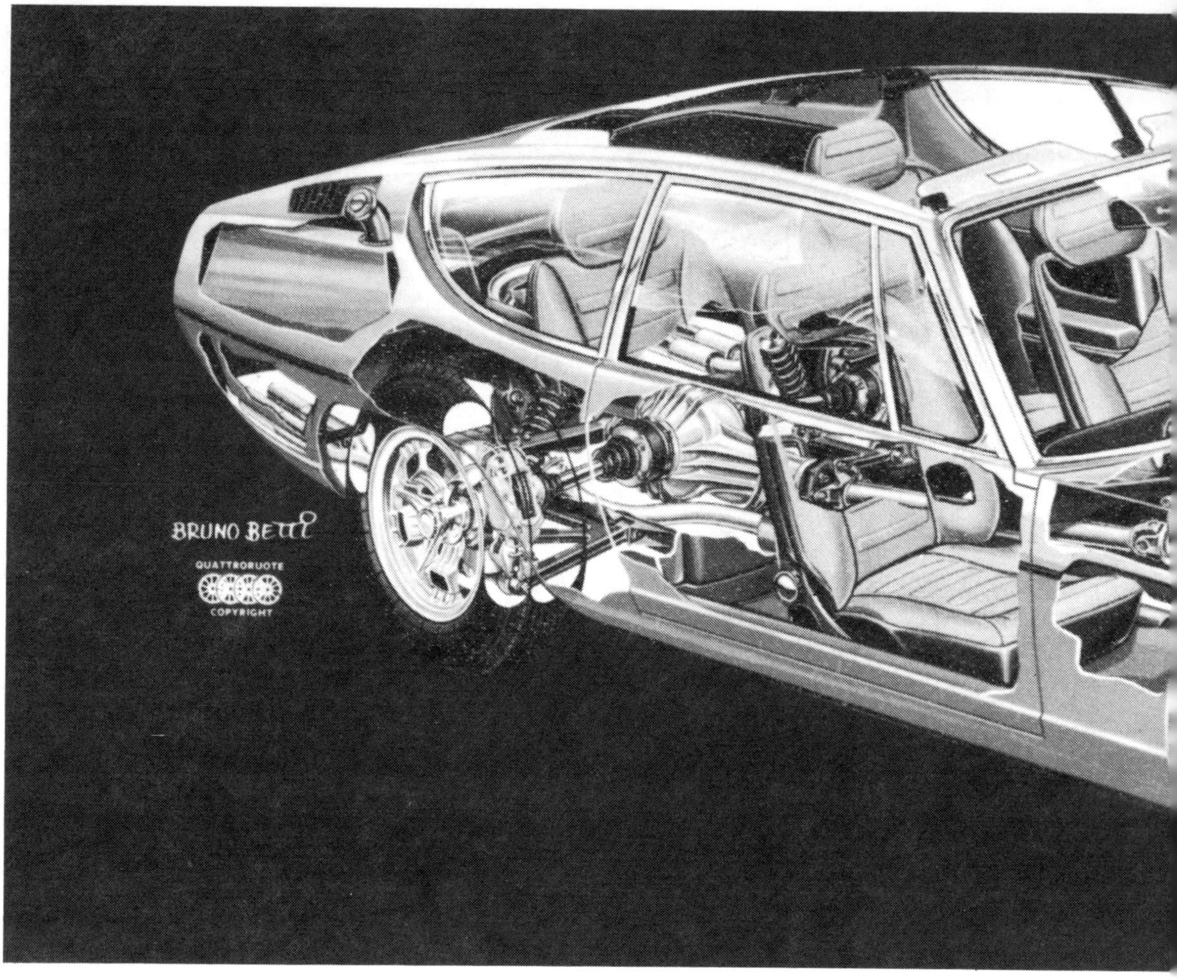

Tecnica d'avanguardia.
Carrozzeria autoportante.
Quattro ruote indipendenti.
Il prestigioso
propulsore Lamborghini V 12
accoppiato ad un cambio
a 5 marce
(anche la retromarcia
è sincronizzata).
Quattro freni a disco
autoventilati.
Accelerazioni poderose.
Tenuta di strada
e maneggevolezza.
Questa
la sicurezza Lamborghini.

Technique d'avant-garde.
Carrosserie autoporteuse.
Quatre roues indépendantes.
La fameuse
mécanique Lamborghini
à 12 cylindres en V
accouplée à une boîte
à 5 vitesses
(la marche arrière
est elle aussi synchronisée)
Quatre freins à disque
autoventilés
à double circuit.
Accélérations fulminantes.
Stabilité
et tenue de route.
Telle est
la sécurité Lamborghini.

Technik im Detail.
Selbsttragende Karrosserie.
Einzelradaufhängung
vorn und hinten.

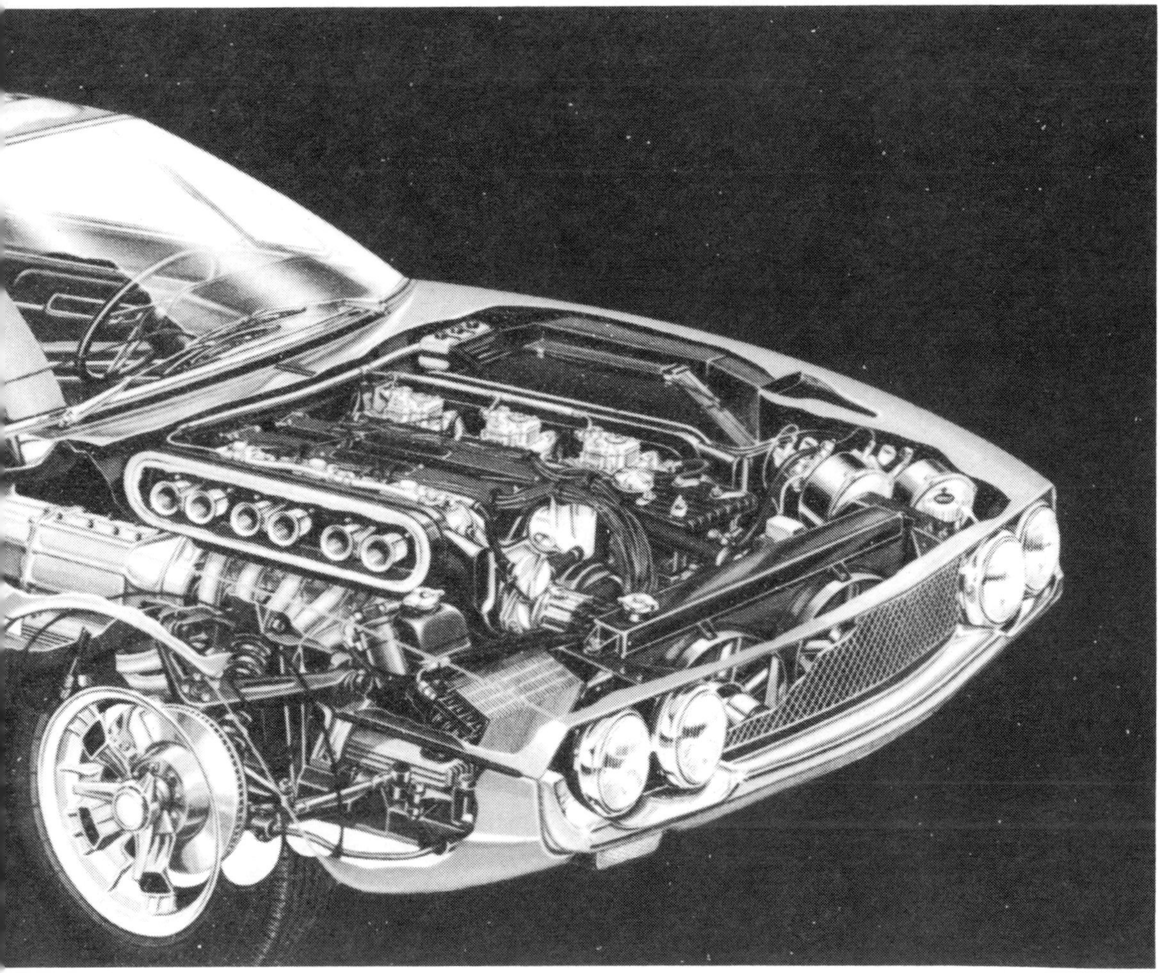

V-12 Hochleistungsmotor.
5-Gang-Vollsynchrongetriebe
Vierrad
Zweikreis ventilierte
Scheibenbremse.
Vollblut Beschleunigungen.
Hervorragende
Richtungsstabilität
und Strassenlage.
So heisst die Espada-Sicherheit.

The full breath
of Lamborghini Espada's appeal.
Bodywork of
monocoque construction.
Independent suspensions
front and rear.
The world famous
Lamborghini V-12 power unit
teamed with
a 5 speed
all syncromeshed gearbox.
Ventilated disc brakes
on all four wheels
with independent circuits
to front and rear.
All-out performances
matched by the highest degree
of handling
and controlability.
That's the Espada safety.

Bodywork
4 seater Coupé (Bertone)
Sumptuous leather upholstery and safety padding
Twin halogen lights
Electrically operated windows - tinted glasses
Laminated windscreen - electrically heated rear window
Trunk capacity 20 cu.ft. - full air conditioning

Engine, transmission
V 12 cylinder (60°)
Capacity 3929 cc (82 x 62 mm) or 240 cu.in. (3.22 x 2.40 in.)
Compression ratio 10.7 : 1
Maximum power 350 bhp (DIN) at 7500 rpm
Maximum torque 40 mkg (290 ft. lbs.) (DIN) at 5500 rpm
Light alloy cylinder-block and heads
7 crankshaft bearings
2 x 2 overhead camshafts
Single ignition system by 1 distributor
6 horizontal twin carburetters Weber 40 DCOE 20-21
Pressurised cooling system: vertical-flow radiator and twin electric fans
Lamborghini 5 speed all syncromesh gearbox
Constant velocity final drive shafts
Electrical equipment 12 V - battery 72 Ah - alternators 2 x 770

Body
All-steel body of integral construction
Independent front and rear suspension consisting of double transverse wishbones with coil springs, telescopic Koni dampers, and anti-roll bars
Girling ventilated disc braking on all four wheels operated by 2 vacuum servo-units with independent circuits to front and rear brakes
Magnesium wheels 7 Jj x 15''
Tyres: Pirelli 215-70 VR 15
Cinturato HS CN 12

Principal dimensions
Wheel base 2650 mm (104.3 in.)
Track front and rear 1490 mm (58.6 in.)
Length 4738 mm (186.5 in.)
Width 1860 mm (73.4 in.)
Height 1185 mm (46.6 in.)
Dry weight 1635 kg (3605 lbs.)

Performances
Top Speed: 250 km/h (155 mph)
Acceleration on 1 standing km.: 26 sec.

Jarama

The Jarama, which was introduced in 1970, succeeded the Islero as Lamborghini's front-engined grand touring sports car. Although it was initially criticized for an interior of mediocre quality and an excessive curb weight, the Jarama's superbly proportioned body was internationnally acclaimed as an outstanding example of excellent design. Key elements of this Bertone creation included prominent front and rear fender arches, a broad hood with twin NACA ducts on its outer surfaces, dual headlights that were semi-enclosed by a retractable fairing when not in operation and a very effective use of what in pre-war years was described as razor-edge styling. The roof line didn't begin to taper downward into the truncated rear deck until well past the rear wheels, thus providing the rear passengers with adequate headroom. Visibility from any seat was excellent through the Jarama's large expanses of glass.

Most of the Jarama's mechanical components were those of the Islero S. Thus its all-independent suspension consisted of unequal length A-arms, coil springs, tubular shocks and anti-roll bars both front and rear. Its internally ventilated disc brakes had an 11.8 inch diameter and, with worm and sector steering, providing 4.5 turns lock to lock. The Jarama's turning circle measured 39.3 feet. Pirelli Cinturato HS215/70-VR15 tires were mounted on 15x7 inch cast aluminum Campagnolo wheels. Initially, these had knock-off hubs but later models were equipped with versions having a bolt-on arrangement.

Although the Jarama's curb weight of 3,600 pounds was unwelcomed, it was, with a 93.5 inch wheelbase, a height of just 46.9 inches and an overall length of 176.5 inches, a very compact automobile. Front and rear tread was 58.7 inches. Driving the rear wheels was the familiar Lamborghini 4 cam V-12 with a displacement of 3929 cc (240 cubic inches). Maximum horsepower and torque were respectively 350(DIN) at 7500 rpm and 289 ft-lb (DIN) at 5500 rpm. A compression ratio of 10.7:1 was claimed and 6 Weber DCOE 20/21, 2-barrel carburetors were fitted. The standard transmission was a 5 speed, all-synchromesh unit and the rear axle ratio was 4.50:1.

Interior appointments were finished in leather and cord cloth and a wood panel insert provided the backdrop for the circular dials which included a 180 mph speedometer, 9000 rpm tachometer, oil pressure, coolant temperature, ammeter, fuel level and clock. Mounted on a sill before the triple-spoked steering wheel were a series of rocker switches (for lighting, heating, etc.). Warning lights for virtually every function and feature were also fitted. Included in the Jarama's $22,500 list price was air conditioning, AM/FM radio-tape deck and electric windows.

In 1972 with the introduction of the S version at the Geneva show, the Jarama became a far more refined sports car. By virtue of altered cylinder heads, carburetion and valve timing, its horsepower was raised to 365. The hood now carried an additional air intake and side vents were installed behind the front wheels. The earlier-mentioned bolt-on magnesium wheels were also introduced on the Jarama S. The quality of the Jarama interior was significantly upgraded and, by virtue of reshaped front seats rear passenger leg room was improved. Both the three-speed, Torqueflite transmission and removable roof panels were Jarama S options. When production ceased in 1978 a total of 250 units of both types had been constructed.

Jarama literature included the 1973 vintage Jarama S catalogue reproduced here (see pages 68-76). There was an earlier Jarama folder and the Jarama was included in at least a couple of full-line Lamborghini brochures.

The JARAMA S 400 GT looks to the future with the most sought after features in advanced technical engineering. A 240 cubic inch, 365 horsepower V-12 engine, independent suspension front and rear, low centre of gravity, light weight and aerodynamic efficiency, provide the ultimate in performance and road holding.

Der LAMBORGHINI JARAMA S ist der jüngste Nachfolger auf der Linie fortschrittlicher, aussergewöhnlicher und zugleich vernünftiger Automobiltechnik. Sein 12-Zylinder-Motor ist organisch in ein Formel-Fahrwerk mit einzeln aufgehängten Rädern und innenbelüfteten Scheibenbremsen integriert. Italienisches Formgefühl und aerodynamische Erkenntnisse zeichnen für die Karosserieform verantwortlich.

L'eleganza e l'esclusività di uno stile che fonde lusso ed estetica, prestigio e personalità, comfort e sicurezza.

L'élégance et l'exclusivité d'un style qui unit le luxe à l'esthétique, le prestige à la personnalité, le confort à la sécurité.

The Jarama S combines distinctive styling and individuality in an oustanding personal motor car that stands unique in the world of sporting and luxury motoring.

Die Harmonie seines Komforts, der rennmässigen Fahrleistungen, des Überangebots an Sicherheit, Exklusivität und reinrassige automobilischen Erlebens stempeln ihn zum echten Grand-Tourismo.

una linea bertone

EE 0
2319

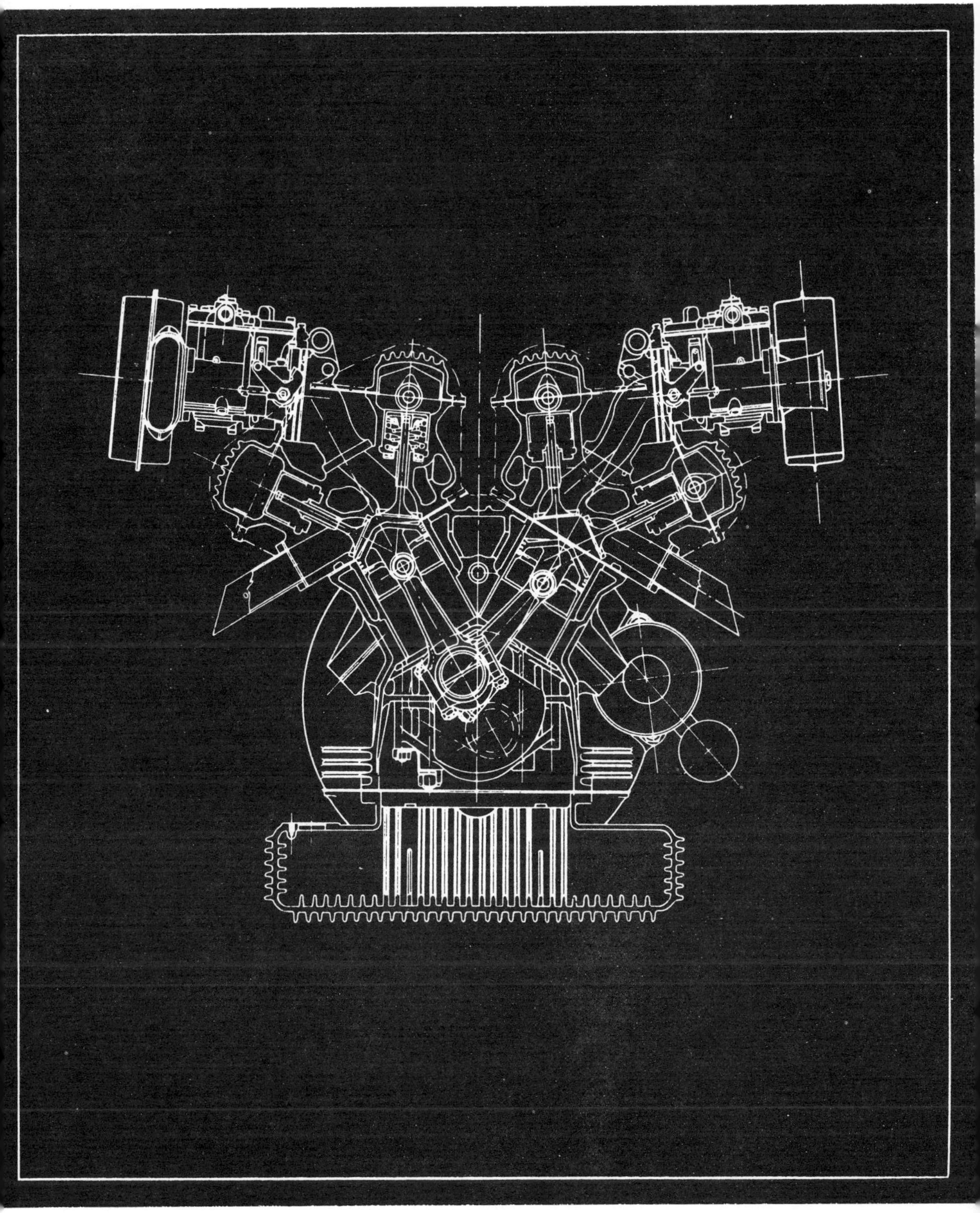

Bodywork

2+2 seater Coupé (Bertone styling)
Sumptuous leather upholstery and safety padding
Twin halogen lights
Electrically operated windows - tinted glasses
Laminated windscreen
Electrically heated rear window
Rear trunk capacity 15,2 cu.ft.
Reclining rear seat providing additional luggage capacity

Engine, transmission

V-12 cylinder (60°)
Capacity 3929 cc (82×62 mm) or 240 cu.in. (3.22×2.40 in.)
Compression ratio 10,7 : 1
Maximum power 365 bhp (DIN) at 7500 rpm
Maximum torque 41,5 mkg (300 ft. lbs) (DIN) at 5500 rpm
Light alloy cylinder block and heads
7 crankshaft bearings
2×2 overhead camshafts
Single ignition system by 1 twin distributor
Feeding by 6 horizontal twin carburetters
Weber 40 DCOE 20-21
Pressurised cooling system: vertical flow radiator and twin electric fans
Lamborghini 5 speed + R all syncromesh gearbox:
Constant velocity final drive shafts
Electrical equipment 12 V - battery 72 Ah - 2 x alternator 770 W

Body

All-steel body of integral construction
Independent suspensions on all four wheels consisting of double transverse wishbones with coil springs, telescopic Koni dampers, and anti-roll bar front and rear
Self ventilating disc braking system (Girling)
on all four wheels hydraulically operated by two vacuum servo-units with independent circuits to front and rear
Magnesium wheels 7JJ × 15"
Low profile tyres Michelin 215-70 VR 15
Pirelli 215-70 VR 15
Cinturato HS CN 12

Principal dimensions

Wheelbase 2380 mm (93.6 in)
Track front and rear 1490 mm (58.6 in.)
Length 4485 mm (176.5 in.)
Width 1820 mm (71.6 in.)
Height 1190 mm (46.8 in.)
Dry weight 1460 kg (340 lbs)

Performances

Top speed: over 260 km/h (162 mph)
Acceleration on 1 standing km: 26 sec.

Countach

The Countach first appeared in March 1971 at the Geneva show as a joint Lamborghini-Bertone idea car. Two years later at Geneva it debuted as a production automobile. Styling of the Countach, by the Bertone designer, Gardini, reflected the primacy of performance in its development. In essence, Gandini was forming the outer skin of a projectile within which mechanical components were given preferential treatment over accommodations for the driver and passenger, The resulting wedge-shaped body was angular, rather than curved and literally bristled with vents, scoops and intakes. A strangely curved rear wheel opening and vertically swinging, gas-supported doors only added fuel to this fire of avant-garde auto design. A huge NACA side scoop plus a pair of vents on the rear deck cooled the Countach's twin vertically-mounted radiators that resided in the rear fenders. Supplying air to the engine were two large scoops just off the cockpit. Nestled between these functional units in a small indentation whose surface was rippled by another series of engine heat extracting vents was the Countach's very small and narrow rear window. The overall impression of the Countach's rear deck was that it had been inspired by a devotee of Aztec architecture! Virtually the only concessions to convention were the triple rear lights (tail, stop and back-up) on either side and for those who weren't sure what had just blasted past, Lamborghini Countach script.

The non-stressed external body components constructed of ultra-thin (1.0 mm) aluminum were riveted to a tubular frame. Some inner body panels were fabricated from an exotic "Avional" superlight alloy. The frame, with its multitude of units, suggested that of the early-sixties Maserati type 60 and 61 sports cars. But of greater importance was the safety feature provided the Countach's occupants, who were effectively sheltered by a strong roll cage.

The Countach's front suspension consisted of unequal-length A-arms, coil springs and shocks with an anti-roll bar placed behind the various suspension components. At the rear, a single, transverse upper link, lower A-arms and twin radius rods were installed. All shock absorbers, including the two per back wheel, were expensive, lightweight Koni units with aluminum cylinder bodies and adjustments for both ride height and stiffness. No rubber bushings were used in the suspension system. Instead, nylon elements were utilized. At all four wheels were Girling 18/4, 4-piston, 10.5 inch disc brakes with ventilated alloy calipers. Their use on the Countach marked the first time they had been installed in a production automobile. Both the Countach's rack and pinion steering (with 3.1 turns lock to lock) and five-speed transmission were Lamborghini designed and built. The limited slip differential was supplied by ZF and the standard rear axle ratio was 4.0:1.

The target weight for the Countach had been 2,205 pounds and at 2,390 pounds the production version came close. Contributing to this achievement was the extensive use of magnesium castings for a large number of components. A partial list includes the following: front and rear hub carriers, steering housing, sump, oil pump and oil filter housing, hand brake calipers, wheels and housings for gearbox and clutch. Respective dimensions of the front and rear Campagnolo wheels were 14x7.5 and 14x9 inches. Corresponding sizes of the standard Michelin XWX tires were 205/70-VR14 and 215/70-VR14.

The prototype Countach had been powered by a 4971 cc (303 cid) version of the Lamborghini dohc V-12. However this 440 horsepower engine was regarded as a bit too fragile for the production version which was released with the V-12 in 3929 cc displacement (240 cid) form with a 3.22 inch bore and 2.40 inch stroke. Six horizontal Weber 45 DCOE, two-barrel carburetors were fitted and ratings of 375 (DIN) hp at 8000 rpm and 268 lb-ft of torque at 5500 rpm were quoted.

Unlike the transverse-position of the Miura's V-12, the Countach's engine was placed in a longitudinal location. However the nose of the engine was at the end of the car! Thus, the transmission (which was directly behind the cockpit) was connected to an enclosed shaft which ran alongside the engine back to the differential which was housed within the engine's oil sump casting.

In comparison to the Countach's sensational styling and advanced engineering, its interior appeared conservative and subdued. A thick, three-spoke steering wheel faced a thin panel in which were installed eight Stewart-Warner gauges. Along with a 320 Km/Hr speedometer and 9000 rpm tachometer were found dials for oil pressure and temperature, coolant temperature, ammeter, voltmeter and fuel level. In addition, eight warning lights monitored such systems and functions as brakes, hand brake, alternator, air conditioning fan and compressor, parking lights, seat belts, hazard lights, high beams and directionals. A good deal of suede was used for the interior appointments and the center console both supported additional switches and provided a sturdy base for the Lamborghini's husky shifter. The two leather finished seats were of the appropriate space-age form.

The Countach was in almost a constant state of evolution but the first major change in its design came in 1977 with the introduction of the LP400S version. Larger and wider Campagnolo cast alloy wheels measuring 15x8 1/2 inches (front) and 15x 12 inches (rear) were installed along with Pirelli 205/50VR-15 (front) and 345/35VR-15 (rear) P7 tires. These new wheels and tires required the addition of fiberglass wheel flares. Those at the front blended into a chin spoiler while the rear versions wrapped around the back deck to terminate between the rear light zones. Other technical changes included the installation of larger, 11 inch diamter disc brakes and a restructuring of the suspension geometry. The LP400S engine ratings were 353 (DIN) hp at 9500 rpm and 267 lb-ft at 5500 rpm. Aside from its wheel-well flares the S version was easily identified by its additional driving lights set low in the bumper which also was fitted with small grilles on its outer panels. The basic format of the Countach interior was unchanged but appointments were generally of a higher caliber and there was more extensive use of leather.

The LP500S was a virtual twin to the 400S model but its engine, displacing 4754 cc, was credited with 400 (DIN) hp at 7000 rpm. Peak torque output was 303 ft-lb at 4500 rpm.

Sales of the Countach in the U.S. required compliance with safety and emission regulations which often pushed its price into the vicinity of $85,000. Output of the LP400 was approximately 300 units and both the 400S and 500S versions are currently available as this book is written.

Countach literature included an introductory folder, a couple of catalogues in the late seventies, a folder in 1981 and a similar 1981 portfolio, which has been reproduced here (see pages 80-90). The Countach was also mentioned in various full-line Lamborghini pieces, including small items from the German and British distributors (see pages 78-79 top and pages 78-79 bottom, respectively).

COUNTACH LP400

Motor:	12 Zylinder V-60° Motor
Hubraum:	3929 ccm
Leistung:	350 PS bei 7500 UpM
Max. Drehmoment:	36,8 kgm bei 5500 UpM
Höchstgeschwindigkeit:	279,6 km/h bei 7500 UpM 5. Gang
Getriebe:	5 Vorwärts-, 1 Rückwärtsgang
Vergaser:	6 Weber Vertikal-Doppelvergaser
Preis:	**DM 178.500,–**

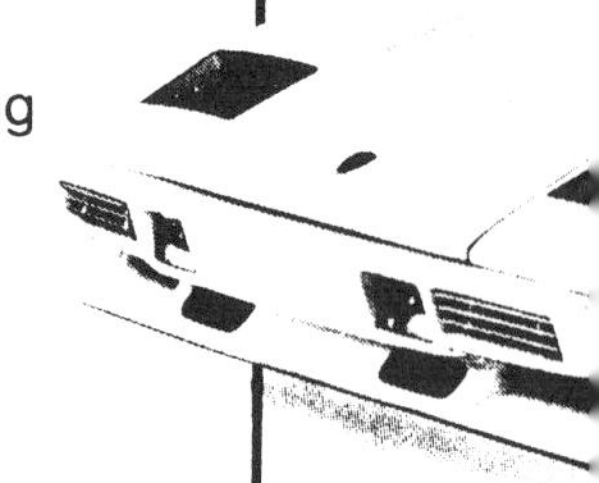

Countache: Not just a one-off design exercise by Bertone. The Lamborghini Countache will be the first practical futuristic car to be put into production by any manufacturer. With a 5 litre engine producing 440 bhp, the Countache will be capable of 200 mph +, making it not only the world's fastest production car, but also the most beautiful and desirable. **Bodywork:** 2 seater berlinetta (Bertone). Spare wheel and battery located in front. Retractable halogen headlights. Laminated windscreen. Tinted glass. **Engine:** V - 12 (60°) longitudinal mid-engine rear located between gearbox and differential (LAMBORGHINI System). Capacity 4971 cc (85x73mm). Compression ratio 10.5:1. Maximum power 440 bhp at 7400 rpm. Light-alloy castings. 7 crankshaft bearings. 2x2 over-head camshafts (chains). Single ignition over 1 twin distributor. 6 hor. twin carburetters Weber 42 DCOE. Pressurised cooling system over 2 crossflow radiators and 2x2 electric fans. **Gear box:** Lamborghini 5+R speed gearbox all syncromesh. Constant velocity final drive shafts. Electrical equipment: 12V - battery 56 Ah - alternator 770 W. **Chassis:** All-steel body of monocoque construction. Independent suspension front and rear consisting of double transverse wishbones with coil springs, telescopic dampers and anti-roll bar front and rear. Ventilated disc braking system with independent circuit to front and rear. Cast magnesium rims: front 7Lx14", rear 9Lx14". Low profile radial tires.

Dimensions: Wheelbase 97" (2450 mm). Track front 58" (1500 mm). Track rear 62" (1520 mm). Length 162" (4010 mm). Width 74" (1870 mm). Height 42" (1030 mm). Curb weight 2492 lbs (1130 kg). **Maximum speed:** 200 mph+ (300 km/h+).

lamborghini

countach S

lamborghini countach

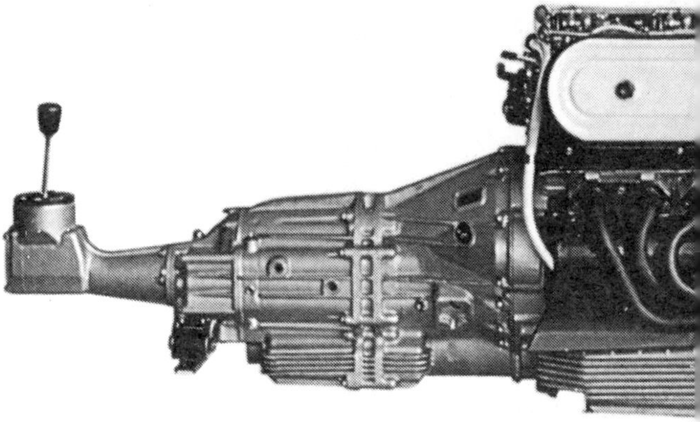

.P400 S

CHAISSIS

Tubular frame of integral construction - Fiberglass floor panels - Light alloy body - 2 Seater Coupé
Track: front 1492 mm - rear 1606 mm - Wheelbase 2450 mm - Lenght 4140 mm - Width 2000 mm
Height 1070 mm - Weight 1400 Kg. - Mid-engine with longitudinal layout - Independent front and rear suspension with transverse A arms, dampers and coaxial springs - Rear suspension with two damper units per wheel - Front and rear stabiliser bars - Constant-moving drive shafts - Rack and pinion steering - Dual circuit hydraulic brakes with servo units and alloy calipers - Brake regulator on rear axle - Ventilated brake discs - Wheels: Elektron rims front 8" 1/2x15 - rear 12"x15 - Tyres: front 205/50 VR 15 Pirelli P 7 - rear 345/35 VR 15 Pirelli P7 - Laminated glass windshield - Adjustable steering wheel - Parallelogramm windshield wipers - Luggage van capacity: lts. 240 - 2 light alloy fuel tanks, total capacity lts. 120

ENGINE

Original Lamborghini design with gearbox mounted ahead of engine - V 12 60° engine - Capacity: 3929 cc^3 - Stroke: 62 mm - Bore: 82 mm - Compression ratio: 10,5:1 - Maximum power: 350 Hp DIN at 7500 rpm - Maximum torque 36,8 Kgm at 5500 rpm. - Ligh alloy cylinder block and heads - 7 bearing crankcase - Timing system: 2 overhead camshafts (chain) - Electronic ignition: single magnetic Marelli distributor - Carburation by six horizontal Weber twin choke 40 DCOE carburettors - Cooling system by two side mounted horizontal flow water radiators and two electric fans - Electrical system: 12 V 72 Ah battery 70 A alternator - Separated oil radiator - Lamborghini all-synchro five speed + reverse gearbox - Ratios: 1st speed: 2,256:1 - 2nd speed: 1,769:1 - 3rd speed: 1,310:1 - 4th speed: 0,990:1 5th speed: 0,775:1 - reverse: 2,134:1 - Axle ratio: 11/45 - Limited slip differential - Single plate dry clutch hydraulically operated.

PERFORMANCES

Speeds attainable at 7500 rpm:
1st speed: 93,6 km/h - 2nd speed: 119,3 km/h - 3rd speed: 161,1 km/h - 4th speed: 213,3 km/h - 5th speed: 279,6 km/h

lamborghini

Urraco

The P250, of which 350 examples were constructed, represented Lamborghini's entry into the class of exotic GT automobiles that in terms of physical size, price and performance was a notch or two below the level of the V-12 Lamborghini and Ferrari models. This segment of the market was hotly contested by Ferrari with its Dino 308 GT4, by the Maserati Merak and by Lamborghini's P250 Urraco, introduced at the 1970 Turin auto show.

Although the Urraco didn't enter into production until 1973, its styling by Bertone remained exciting and contemporary. Retractable headlights were mounted fairly far up along the fender line and the slightly recessed hood area carried twin vents for the cooling system. In profile, the Urraco's front end had a bullet-like form as the long and narrow grille opening served as the junction of the converging hood and lower fender lines. On European models an extremely graceful and delicate chrome bumper surrounded the upper grille line and embraced the dual running lights. The more rigorous U.S. market regulations required installation of a larger, black-finish version. To provide reasonable, if not spacious, accommodations for the Urraco's rear seat occupants, its roofline ran nearly the body's full length, joining the high-mounted rear deck in a very harmonious fashion. Very simple rectangular tail-lights (two on each side) and quadruple exhausts (also two to a side) plus thin bumper strips provided a subdued backdrop for the Urraco's black slatted rear window. The rear bumpers on U.S. models were considerably larger but remained well integrated into the Urraco's overall styling theme. Giving the Urraco virtually instant recognition were black engine intake louvers on the rear quarter panels. Key dimensions of the Urraco included a 96.5 inch wheelbase, overall length of 167.3 inches, a width of 69.3 inches and a 43.9 inch height. Both front and rear track was 57.5 inches. A front trunk provided accommodations for the spare tire, tools and air conditioning unit. Behind the engine was a 5.6 cubic foot trunk.

Standard equipment included in the Urraco's 1975 U.S. sticker price of $22,500 included air conditioning, electric windows, tinted glass, leather upholstery and an AM/FM radio. The two circular air conditioning outlets were mounted vertically on a panel in front of the center console. A deeply dished steering wheel with four spokes was placed midway between the Urraco's instruments. Large tachometer and speedometer dials were mounted at the panel's extreme right and left, respectively, and six warning lights separated the same number of gauges into two sections.

The Urraco's monocoque body was based upon a sheet-steel platform and a sub-frame carried the engine, transmission and rear suspension. An all-independent suspension with MacPherson struts, a lower A-arm, large anti-roll bar and coil springs with integral tube shock absorbers at the front and a similar arrangement at the rear gave the Urraco exceptional cornering power. Non-power 10.9 inch vented disc brakes were used front and rear and 14 inch Campagnolo bolt-on wheels with 7 inch rims were fitted with 205VR, low-profile Michelin tires.

Translated into English, Urraco became "Little Bull" and this term aptly described its transversely-mounted, mid-ship located, V-8 engine. Constructed, with the exception of steel cylinder liners, totally of aluminum, it weighed just 375 pounds (without manifolds but equipped with all accessories). A single overhead cam per cylinder bank, operated by a toothed belt, controlled the valves and, with a bore and stroke of 3.39 and 2.09 inches, total displacement was 150 cubic inches or 2463 cc. Horsepower and torque ratings were 220 hp at 7500 rpm and 166 ft-lb at 5750 rpm. Four Weber 40IDF-1 vertically mounted carburetors were fitted and the compression ratio was 10.5:1. A 4.25:1 rear axle was standard and the five-speed, all-synchromesh gearbox along with the transmission and differential had a light-alloy housing.

In addition to the P111 version for the U.S. market, two other forms of the Urraco, the P200 and P300 were produced. The former had a smaller 1994 cc displacement by virtue of a reduced 77.4 mm instead of 86 mm bore and four Weber 40DCNF carburetors. Its maximum horsepower was 182 at 7800 rpm. Peak torque was 131 lb-ft at 5750 rpm. A 4.0:1 rear axle was specified and Michelin XWX 205/70VR-14 tires were mounted on 7.5 inch rims. Approximately 80 examples of this version were built.

The P300 Urraco had a 3 liter engine (86 mm bore, 64.5 mm stroke) the same Weber carburetors of the P200 and a 250 hp at 7800 rpm rating. Maximum torque was 195 lb-ft at 5750 rpm. The location of its headlights was placed further forward. With a top speed in excess of 160 mph and a zero to 60 mph time of 6.5 seconds, the P300 was the most potent example of the Urraco, which, after a production run of just over 600 cars, was phased out during 1977.

There was an early Urraco catalogue printed by Renografica-Bologna that illustrated exterior photos only, but the main Urraco catalogues were those issued in 1973, 1975 and 1976 on, respectively, the P250 (see pages 92-104), P300 (see pages 116-126) and 111 (see pages 105-115). The P300 catalogue was issued in at least three different editions and the various Urraco models found their way into other full-line Lamborghini brochures, as well.

urraco
P250

urraco P250 lamborghini

Lamborghini URRACO:
una berlinetta a quattro posti, di cilindrata media
e dalle prestazioni elevatissime,
con il gruppo propulsore sistemato in posizione centrale
davanti all'asse delle ruote posteriori.
Erede degli avanzati concetti tecnici della Casa
l'URRACO è una vettura non solo impostata su prestazioni eccezionali
intese in senso assoluto, bensi su qualità non meno importanti,
quali il comfort e la praticità,
che ne rendono la guida piacevole e comoda
anche nelle più svariate condizioni d'uso.

Lamborghini URRACO:
Berlinette quatre places, à cylindrée moyenne et performances très élevées.
Le moteur central est placé transversalement en avant de l'axe des roues arrière.
Confort et aisance de conduite complètent les caractéristiques de cette voiture, expression la plus récente des traditions d'avant-garde de Lamborghini.

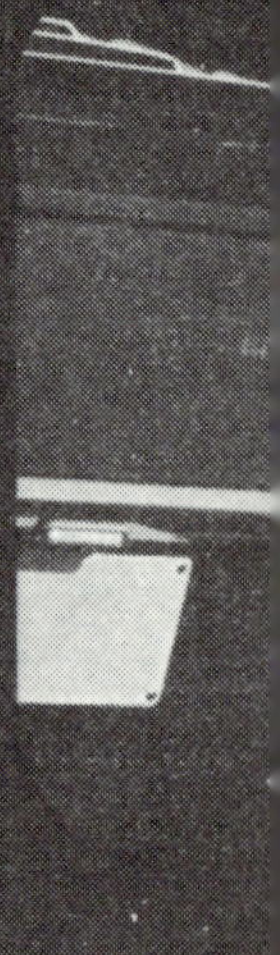

The Lamborghini URRACO:
A high performance mid engined
four seater "Berlinetta"
with medium cubic capacity.
Successor to the advanced technical
designs incorporated in the 350 and 400 GT 2+2,
the URRACO offers outstanding performance
and road holding,
combined with all round versatility.

Lamborghini URRACO:
4-sitzige "Berlinetta" mittlerer Groesse.
Der Mittelmotor
gewährleistet höchste Leistungen.
Erbe der fortschrittlichen technischen
Lösungen des Lamborghini - Werkes,
bietet dieser Wagen ausserdem
einmaligen Komfort unter
den verschiedensten Fahrbedingungen.

una linea bertone

Disegnata da Bertone,
la LAMBORGHINI URRACO è slanciata e al tempo stesso molto compatta.
La sua linea frutto di profonde ricerche stilistiche
soddisfa le esigenze aerodinamiche
imposte dalle eccezionali prestazioni e quelle inedite dalla vettura,
spiccatamente sportiva a motore posteriore centrale,
di notevole abitabilità.

BO 348

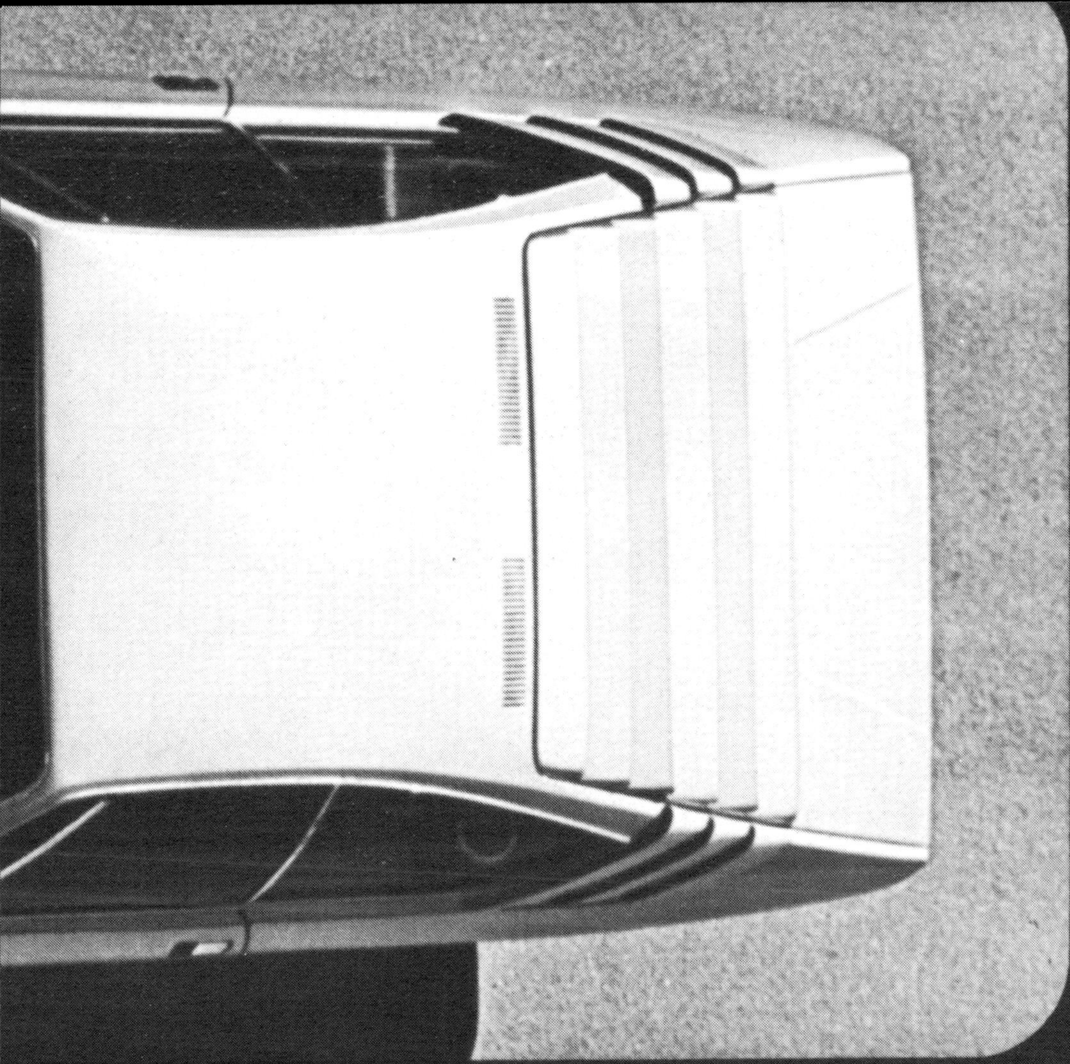

Dessinée par Bertone,
la URRACO a une ligne aérodynamique
et en même temps compacte.
Résultat d'études avancées, elle offre,
avec des performances nettement sportives,
une mécanique raffinée
et un habitacle spacieux.

The URRACO, with its Bertone designed body,
is both streamlined and compact.
The many innovative features
of the car include an aerodynamic body
which combines comfort to complement
the car's outstanding performance.

Von Bertone entworfen,
weist der URRACO eine schlanke
und zugleich kompakte Linienführung auf.
Ein ausserordentliches stylistisches
Empfinden vereint Stromlinienaufbau
mit höchsten Leistungen,
Fahrkomfort mit sportlichem Elan.

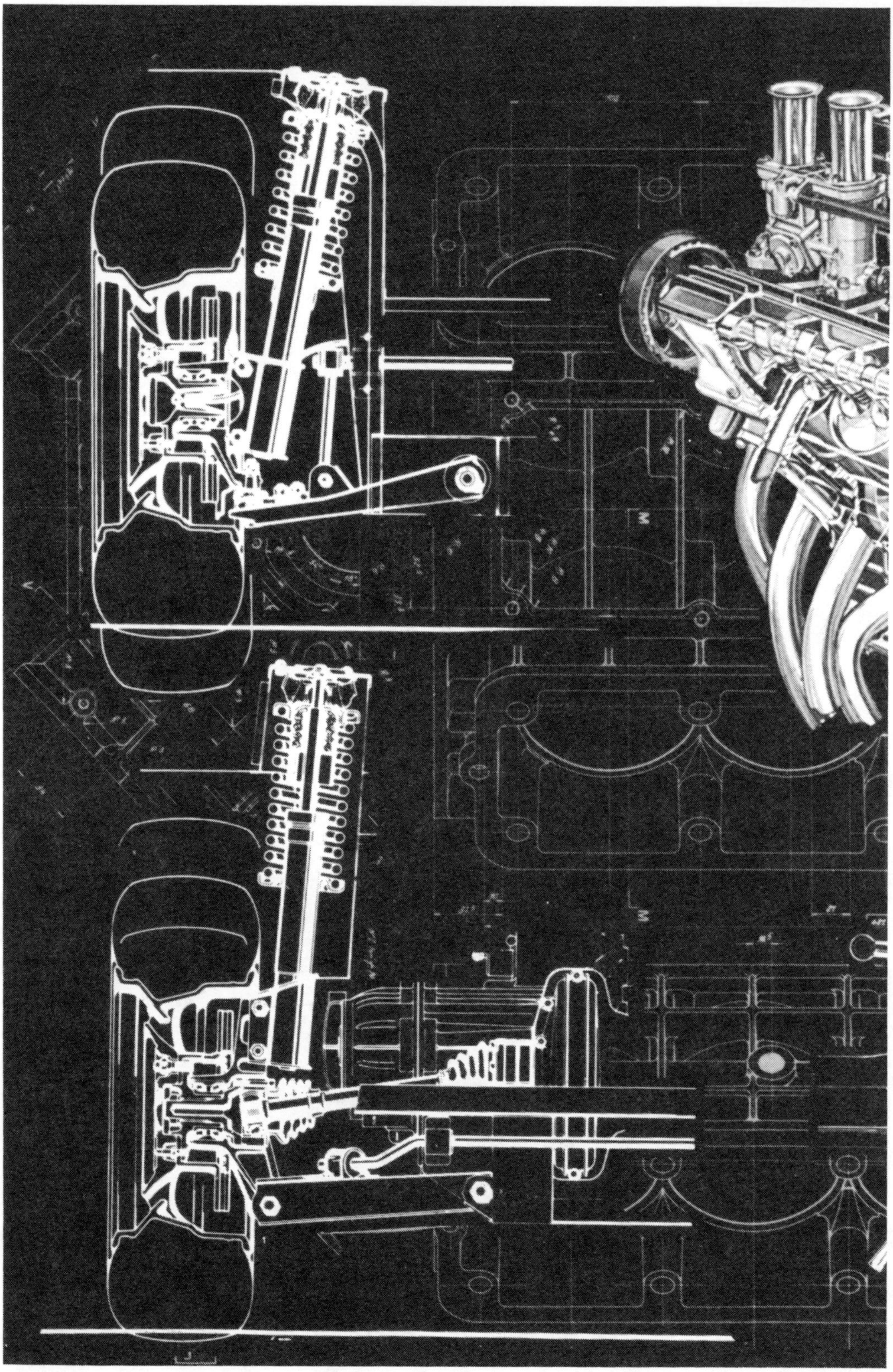

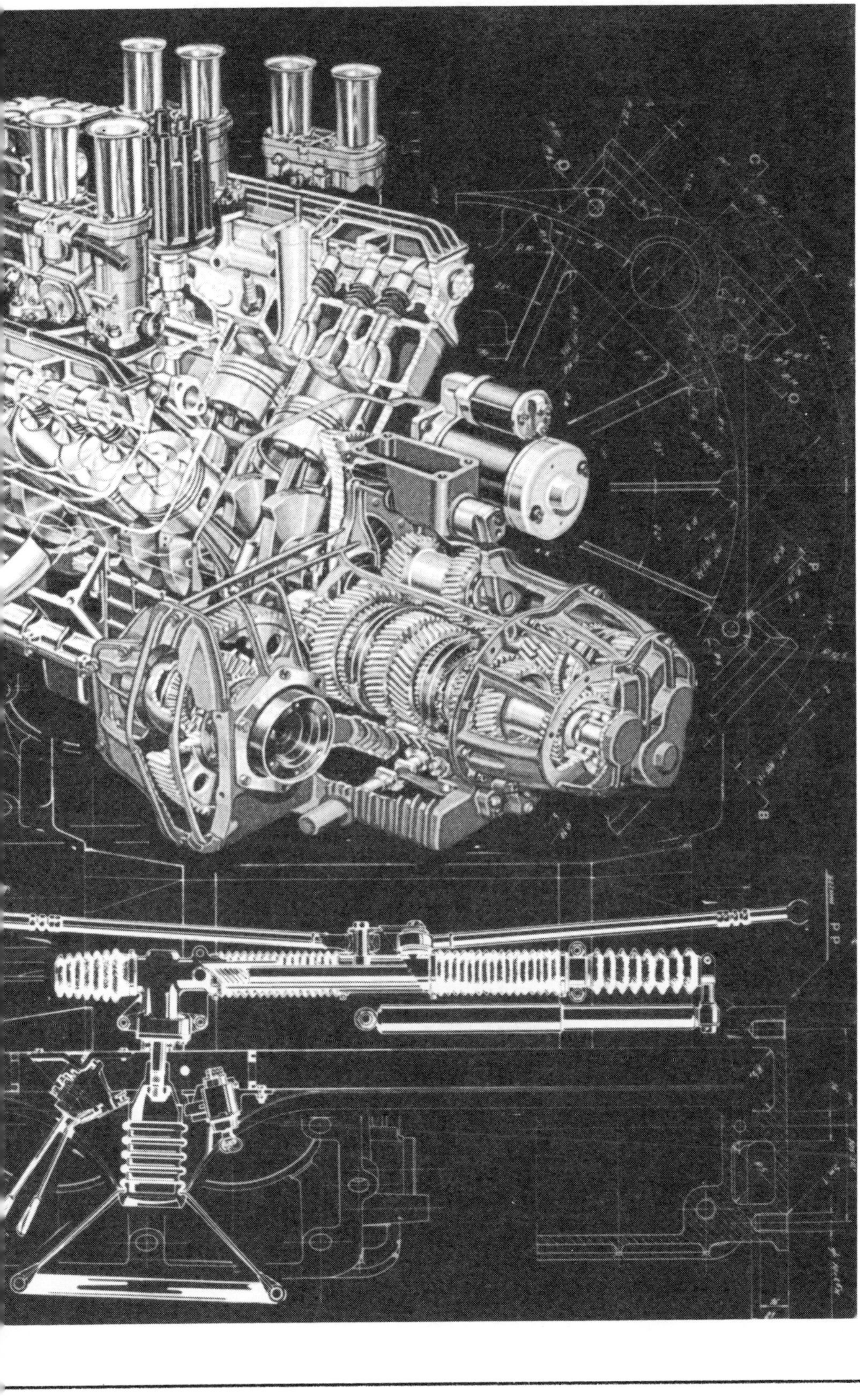

LAMBORGHINI URRACO P 250

Engine and transmission
Engine: V 8 at 90°
Displacement: 2463 cm^3 (86x53)
Compression ratio: 10.4 : 1
Maximum horsepower: 220 HP (DIN)
Maximum torque: 23 Mkg.
Maximum RPM: 7500
Engine location: central-transverse
Block and heads: Light alloy
Main bearings: 5
Ignition: one distributor and 2x1 coils
Spark plugs: Bosh 235 P 21
Fuel pump: 1 Bendix electric pump 12 V
Carburation: 4 twin - choke carburettors
Lubrication: gear pump
Cooling System: water-cooling by means of a centrifugal pump and of 2 electric fans (one of them with a thermal contact)

Electrical system
Voltage: 12 V
Battery: 55 Amp.
Alternator: Bosch 770 W

Clutch
Single dry disc

Gearbox
Lamborghini 5 speeds + reverse

Transmission
Half-shafts with constant-moving joints

Chassis
Body: monocoque-type
Front suspension: Mc Pherson
Rear suspension: Mc Pherson
Both with anti-roll bars
Brakes: twin-circuit ventilated brakes
Steering: rack-and-pinion-type
Wheels: magnesium alloy - 7.5"x14"
Tyres: radial, low profile 205/70 VR 14 type

Body
4 seater coupé (Bertone)
Lenght: 4250
Width: 1760
Height: 1115 mm
Wheelbase: 2450 mm
track front and rear: 1460 mm
trunk capacity: 285 lt.

Weight
Dry weight (with oil and water): 1100 kos

Performance
Max speed: over 150 mph
Acceleration on standing km (with 2 Passengers): 26,8"

LAMBORGHINI URRACO 111

Engine and transmission
Engine: V 8 at 90°
Displacement: 2463 cm³ (86x53)
Compression ratio: 10.4:1
Maximum horsepower: 180 HP (DIN)
Maximum torque: 20 Mkg.
Maximum RPM: 7500
Engine location: central-transverse
Block and heads: Light alloy
Main bearings: 5
Ignition: one distributor and 1 coil
Spark plugs: Bosh 235 P 21
Fuel pump: 1 Bendix electric pump 12 V
Carburation: 4 twin - choke carburettors
Lubrication: gear pump
Cooling System: water-cooling by means of a centrifugal pump and of 3 electric fans (two of them with a thermal contact)

Electrical system
Voltage: 12 V
Battery: 55 Amp
Alternator: Bosch 770 W

Clutch
Single dry disc

Gearbox
Lamborghini 5 speeds + reverse

Transmission
Half-shafts with constant-moving joints

Chassis
Body: monocoque type
Front suspension: Mc Pherson
Rear suspension Mc Pherson
Both with anti-roll bars
Brakes: twin-circuit ventilated brakes
Steering: rack-and-pinion-type
Wheels: magnesium alloy - 7,5"x14"
Tyres: radial,low profile 205/70 VR 14 type

Body
4 seater coupé (Bertone)
Lenght: 4440 mm.
Width: 1740 mm.
Height: 1160 mm.
Wheelbase: 2450 mm.
Track front 1450 mm., rear 1470 mm.
Trunk capacity: 285 lt.

Weight
Dry weight (with oil and water): 1300 kos.

Performance
Max speed: 140 mph.
Acceleration on standing km (with 2 Passengers): 26,8"

urraco
111

urraco 111 lamborghini

The Lamborghini URRAÇO:
A high performance mid engined
four seater "Berlinetta"
with medium cubic capacity.
Successor to the advanced technical
designs incorporated in the 350 and 400 GT 2+2,
the **URRACO** offers outstanding performance
and road holding,
combined with all round versatility.

design bertone

The URRACO, with its Bertone designed body, is both streamlined and compact. The many innovative features of the car include an aerodynamic body which combines comfort to complement the car's outstanding performance.

lamborghini

urraco
P300

urraco P300 lamborghini

Lamborghini URRACO:
una berlinetta a quattro posti, di cilindrata media
e dalle prestazioni elevatissime,
con il gruppo propulsore sistemato in posizione centrale
davanti all'asse delle ruote posteriori.
Erede degli avanzati concetti tecnici della Casa
l'URRACO è una vettura non solo impostata su prestazioni eccezionali
intese in senso assoluto, bensì su qualità non meno importanti,
quali il comfort e la praticità,
che ne rendono la guida piacevole e comoda
anche nelle più svariate condizioni d'uso.

Lamborghini URRACO:
Berlinette quatre places, à cylindrée moyenne et performances très élevées.
Le moteur central est placé transversalement en avant de l'axe des roues arrière.
Confort et aisance de conduite complètent les caractéristiques de cette voiture, expression la plus récente des traditions d'avant-garde de Lamborghini.

The Lamborghini URRACO:
A high performance mid engined four seater "Berlinetta" with medium cubic capacity.
Successor to the advanced technical designs incorporated in the 350 and 400 GT 2+2, the URRACO offers outstanding performance and road holding, combined with all round versatility.

Lamborghini URRACO:
4-sitzige "Berlinetta" mittlerer Groesse.
Der Mittelmotor gewährleistet höchste Leistungen.
Erbe der fortschrittlichen technischen Lösungen des Lamborghini - Werkes, bietet dieser Wagen ausserdem einmaligen Komfort unter den verschiedensten Fahrbedingungen.

una linea bertone

Disegnata da Bertone,
la LAMBORGHINI URRACO è slanciata e al tempo stesso molto compatta.
La sua linea frutto di profonde ricerche stilistiche
soddisfa le esigenze aerodinamiche
imposte dalle eccezionali prestazioni e quelle inedite dalla vettura,
spiccatamente sportiva a motore posteriore centrale,
di notevole abitabilità.

Dessinée par Bertone,
la URRACO a une ligne aérodynamique
et en même temps compacte.
Résultat d'études avancées, elle offre,
avec des performances nettement sportives,
une mécanique raffinée
et un habitacle spacieux.

The URRACO, with its Bertone designed body,
is both streamlined and compact.
The many innovative features
of the car include an aerodynamic body
which combines comfort to complement
the car's outstanding performance.

Von Bertone entworfen,
weist der URRACO eine schlanke
und zugleich kompakte Linienführung auf.
Ein ausserordentliches stylistisches
Empfinden vereint Stromlinienaufbau
mit höchsten Leistungen,
Fahrkomfort mit sportlichem Elan.

LAMBORGHINI URRACO P 300

Engine and transmission
Engine V 8 at 90
Displacement: 2996 cm (86x64,5)
Compression ratio: 10:1
Maximum horsepower: 250 HP (DIN)
Maximum torque: 27 Mkg - 3500 R.P.M.
Maximum RPM. 7500
Engine location: central-transverse
Block and heads: Light alloy
Main bearings: 5
Ignition: one distributor and 2x1 coils
Spark plugs: Bosh 235 P 21
Fuel pump: 1 Bendix electric pump 12 V
Carburation: 4 twin - choke carburettors
Lubrication: gear pump
Cooling System: water cooling by means of a centrifugal
pump and of 2 electric fans
(one of them with a thermal contact)

Electrical system
Voltage: 12 V
Battery: 55 Amp.
Alternator: Bosch 770 W

Clutch
Single dry disc

Gearbox
Lamborghini 5 speeds + reverse

Transmission
Half-shafts with constant-moving joints

Chassis
Body: monocoque-type
Front suspension: Mc Pherson
Rear suspension: Mc Pherson
Both with anti-roll bars
Brakes: twin-circuit ventilated brakes
and 2 power brakes
Steering: rack-and-pinion-type
Wheels: magnesium alloy - 7.5"x14"
Tyres: radial, low profile (Front 195/70 VR 14)
(Rear 205/70 VR 14)

Body
4 seater coupé (Bertone)
Lenght: 4285 mm.
Width: 1740 mm.
Height: 1160 mm.
Wheelbase: 2450 mm.
Track front 1450 mm., rear 1470 mm.
Trunk capacity: 285 lt.

Weight
Dry weight (with oil and water): 1300 kos

Performance
Max speed: over 162 mph
Acceleration on standing km (with 2 Passengers): 25.8"

Silhouette

The Silhouette which, with its removable fiberglass roof panels qualified as the first open Lamborghini to enter production, was a derivative of the P300 Urraco. Introduced at the 1976 Geneva Salon, it had a short (through 1977) and limited (only 52 were manufactured) production run.

Aside from its Targa roof, the Silhouette's appearance differed from that of the Urraco in many ways. There were no rear quarter panel windows and in place of the Urraco's rounded wheel wells the Silhouette featured flared and squared openings for the tires. In addition, a front spoiler with inset lights, an engine oil cooler and air scoops for the front brakes were installed. For this new model, Campagnolo provided sensational magnesium wheels with a unique "five-cylinder" design. At the front, these wheels measured 15x8 inches with 15x11 inch versions installed at the rear. Respective sizes for the Silhouette's Pirelli P7 tires were 195/50VR-15 (front) and 285/40VR-15 (rear). Found under the small front hood opening was a limited use, Michelin 105X-18X tire mounted on a narrow wheel.

With the exception of stiffer springs and shocks and heavier anti-roll bars, the Silhouette suspension was identical to the Urraco's. Thus, the front suspension consisted of MacPherson struts, lower A-arms, compliance struts, coil springs, tube shocks and an anti-roll bar. Rack and pinion steering with four turns lock to lock was installed and 10.9 inch vertical disc brakes with a vacuum assist were used at all four wheels. Key dimensions of the steel unit body-frame Silhouette included a 96.5 inch wheelbase, front and rear track of 58.3 inches and 60.5 inches, an overall length of 173.2 inches and a height of 43.9 inches. Compared to the Urraco, the Silhouette was 4.7 inches longer and 2 inches lower. With a displacement of 2996 cc (183 cubic inches) the Silhouette's dohc V-8 with a 10.0:1 compression ratio developed 260 (DIN) hp at 7500 rpm. At 3500 rpm its maximum torque of 208 ft-lb was developed. A five-speed manual transmission was standard, as was a 4.00:1 rear axle ratio.

Replacing the widely scattered instrumentation arrangement of the Urraco was a higher positioned Silhouette panel cluster with all gauges closely gathered together. Superceding the Urraco's shelf-mounted rocker switches were toggle switches placed on a center panel.

There was only one important Silhouette brochure, a catalogue issued in 1977 and printed by Stayer-Graph Granarolo. It is reproduced in this chapter (see pages 128-136).

silhouette

silhouette

LAMBORGHINI SILHOUETTE

Una berlinetta dalle prestazioni superiori.
Un invito al piacere della guida che ogni sportivo può assaporare comodamente seduto in speciali poltroncine avvolgibili.
Comfort ed estrema abitabilità si fondono armoniosamente mentre alcune note selettive comprendono i nuovi pneumatici P 7 ed il tettuccio amovibile collocabile all'interno dell'abitacolo.

Une berlinette aux performances supérieures.
Une invitation au plaisir de conduire que chaque sportif peut goûter confortablement assis sur des sièges enveloppants.
Aisance de conduite et extrême habitabilité se fondent d'une manière armonieuse, tandis que parmi certains détails sélectionnés on remarque les nouveaux pneus P 7 et le toit amovible qui peut se placer dans l'habitacle.

A high performance "Berlinetta", an invitation to the pleasure of driving that all sporting enthousiast can experience from their comfortable wraparound seats.
Excellent road-holding blends with extreme habitability.
Selected details among many others are the new P-7 tyres and the removable top which can be stored in the passenger compartment.

Eine "Berlinetta" mit überdurchschnittlichen Leistungen, eine Aufforderung zum Fahrvergnuegen das alle Autoliebhaber erleben können aus ihrer bequemen Lage in speziellen anatomischen Sitzen.
Komfort ist mit äusserster Wohnbarkeit gepaart, während unter den vielen ausgewählten Details die P7-Reifen und der abnehmbare und im Passagierraum zu verstauende Dach zu erwähnen sind.

LAMBORGHINI SILHOUETTE

Engine and transmission
Engine V 8 at 90°
Displacement: 2996 cm (86x64,5)
Compression ratio: 10:1
Maximum horsepower: 250 HP (DIN)
Maximum torque: 27 Mkg - 3500 R.P.M.
Maximum RPM: 7500
Engine location: central-transverse
Block and heads: Light alloy
Main bearings: 5
Ignition: one distributor and 2x1 coils
Spark plugs: Bosch 235 P 21
Fuel pump: 1 Bendix electric pump 12 V
Carburation: 4 twin - choke carburettors
Lubrication: oil gearpump + circuit
inserted radiator and thermostat
Cooling System: water cooling by means of a centrifugal
pump and of 2 electric fans
(one of them with a thermal contact)

Electrical system
Voltage: 12 V
Battery: 55 Amp.
Alternator: Bosch 770 W

Clutch
Single dry disc

Gearbox
Lamborghini 5 speeds + reverse

Transmission
Half-shafts with constant-moving joints

Chassis
Body: monocoque-type
Front suspension: Mc Pherson
Rear suspension: Mc Pherson
Both with anti-roll bars
Brakes: twin-circuit ventilated brakes
and 2 power brakes
Steering: rack-and-pinion-type
Wheels: 8"x15" front
11"x15" rear
P7 tyres: 195/50 VR15 front
285/40 VR15 rear

Body
Two-seater, convertible
Lenght: 4320 mm.
Width: 1880 mm.
Height: 1120 mm.
Wheelbase: 2450 mm.
Track front 1490 mm., rear 1550 mm.
Trunk capacity: 285 lt.

Weight
Dry weight (with oil and water): 1200 kgs

Performance
Max speed: over 162 mph.
Acceleration on standing km (with 2 Passengers): 24"

silhouette
lamborghini

Jalpa

A revamped Silhouette, the Jalpa TP350S, was introduced at Geneva in 1981. Although small styling refinements such as a reshaped B-pillar and magnesium wheels with a turbine-wheel design gave the Jalpa visual identity, the primary distinction between the two models was the Jalpa's larger engine. Its midship-positioned V-8 with overhead cams for each cylinder bank displaced 3488 cc (213 cubic inches) and it developed 250 hp at 7000 rpm. Peak torque was 235 ft-lb at 3250 rpm. The Jalpa shared its suspension system with the Silhouette and the Urraco and its Pirelli P7 tires measured 205?55VR-16 (front) and 225/50VR-16 (rear). These tires were mounted on 16x7 1/2 inch Campagnolo wheels.

Included in the Jalpa's list price of approximately $58,000 were leather seats and upholstery, air conditioning, AM/FM stereo-cassette, electric window lifts and an electrically-controlled mirror on the driver's side. As had been the case with the Silhouette, the Jalpa's Targa top was stowed vertically behind the seats when not in use. The collapsible spare tire was stored in the front hood compartment and 8 cubic feet of luggage space was available in the rear trunk behind the engine. At the present time the Jalpa remains in production.

The Jalpa was covered in a small catalogue (see pages 138-143).

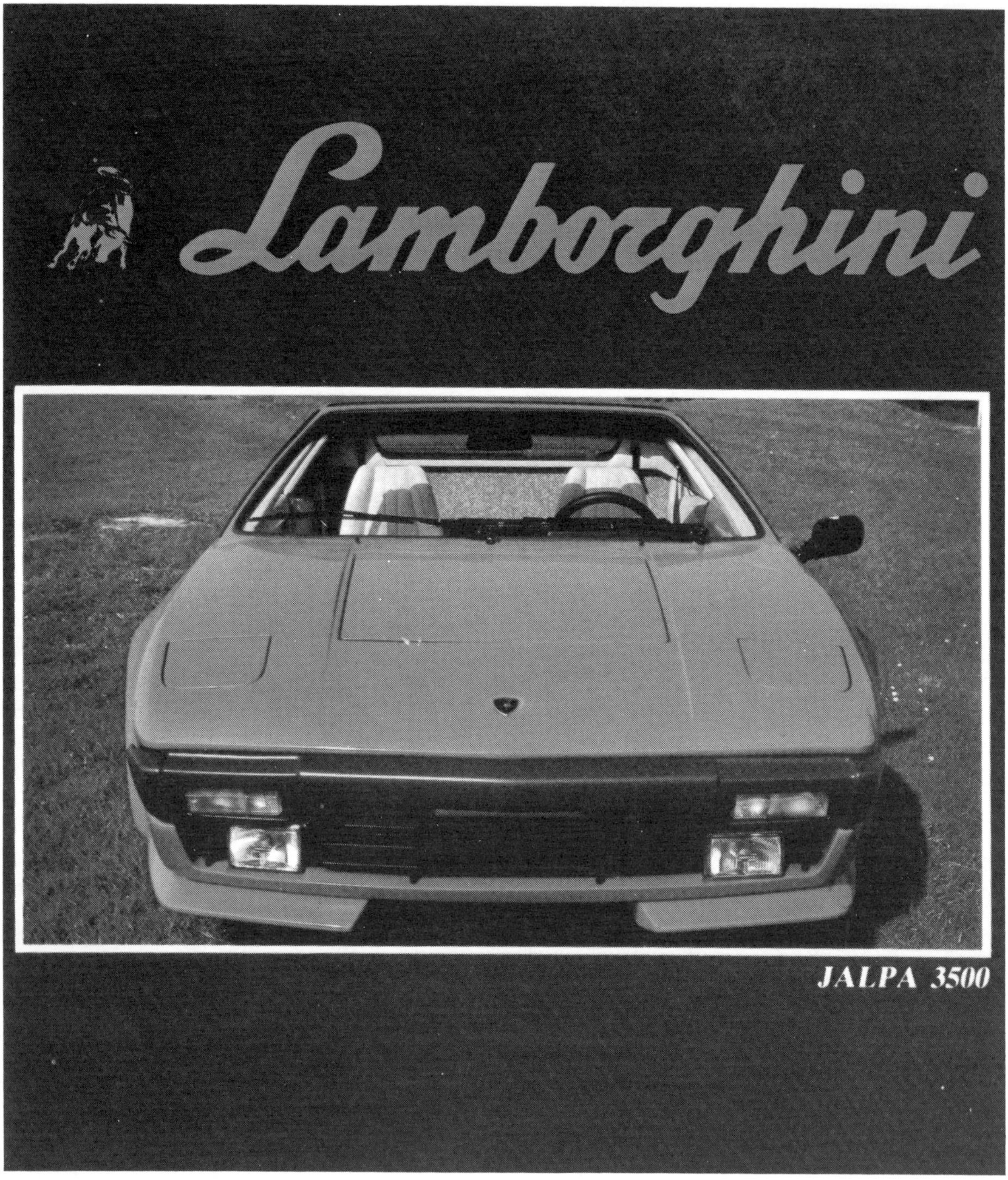
Lamborghini
JALPA 3500

JALPA 3500

LAMBORGHINI JALPA 3500

• Make Nuova Automobili Ferruccio Lamborghini S.p.A. • Model Jalpa • Engine capacity : 3 485 cc • Seats : 2 • Speed at 7 400 rpm : 248 km/h.

Engine • Location rear, transversal • Type fuel engine • Cyclinders : V 8 • Bore and stroke : 86 × 75 cm • Compression ratio : 9,2 : 1 • Max. power (DIN) : 255 HP at 7 000 rpm • Max. torque (DIN) : 32 kgm. at 3 500 rpm • Max. engine r.p.m. : 7 400 • Specific power : 73 HP/l • Cylinder block light alloy • Cylinder head light alloy • Crankshaft bearings : 5 • Valves : 2 overhead for each cylinder • Cam shafts : 2 overhead.

Lubrication • Pump gear type • Filter cartridge type • Lubricating system capacity : 9 liters (with filter).

Carburation • Carburators : 4 • Make, type and further details : Weber 42 DCNF • Feeding electric pump • Cooling system water • Cooling system capacity : 15 liters.

Transmission • Driving wheels : 2, rear • Clutch single plate • Gearbox mechanical, 5. speed + reverse, all synchromesh • Gearbox ratios : 1 : 15/42. 2 : 19/40. 3 : 23/34. 4 : 27/32. 5 : 31/27. Reverse : 15/19 × 21/46. • Gear lever shift type • Differential ratio : 17/68.

Chassis deep-drawing sheet • Front suspensions independent wheels • Rear suspensions independent wheels.

Steering rack-type, no power steering • Turns of steering wheel lock to lock : 4.

Brakes disc type, with booster.

Electrical equipment 12 Volts • Battery : 55 Ah • Generator type : Alternator • Distributor Bosch-magnetic • Headlamps : 2.

Dimensions and weight • Wheel base : 2 450 mm • Front track : 1 500 mm • Rear track : 1 554 mm • Overall lenght : 4 330 mm • Overall width : 1 880 mm • Overall height : 1 140 mm • Ground clearance : 140 mm • Dry weight : 1 510 kg • Distribution of weight : 41 % front axle, 59 % rear axle • Turning dia. : 11 m. • Width of rims : 7,5" • Tyres : 225/50 VR 16 rear, 205/55 VR 16 front • Fuel tank capacity : 80 liters.

Body open • Doors : 2, separate.

Performances • Speeds at 7 000 rpm : 73 km/h in 1st gear, 97 km/h in 2nd gear, 138 km/h in 3rd gear, 172 km/h in 4th gear, 234 km/h in 5th gear. • Power - weight ratio : 6,3 HP/Kg • Carrying capacity : 225 Kg • Speed in 5th gear at 1 000 rpm : 33,5 km/h.

Practical instructions • Fuel Super gasoline • Oil sump capacity : 9 liters • SAE degrees : 10 W 50 API-SF/cc HIL/L/46155 Level • Oil change every 7 000 kms • Gearbox capacity : 3,5 liters • SAE degrees : 85 W/90 • Oil change every 60 000 kms • Tappet clearances - inlet : 0,30 mm, exhaust : 0,40 mm • Valve timing : inlet opens at 32° before t.d.c. and closes at 60° after b.d.c. Exhaust opens at 60° before b.d.c. and closes at 32° after t.d.c. • Normal tyre pressure : front 2,5 atm, rear 2,5 atm.

Specifications may be changed without notice.